in this place

The National Library of Wales

in this place

The National Library of Wales

TREVOR FISHLOCK

ISBN:
Softback 978-1-86225-056-7
Hardback 978-1-86225-054-3

Text: © Trevor Fishlock
Design: Olwen Fowler
Images: Collections of The National Library of Wales
www.llgc.org.uk

100 LlGC NLW Llyfrgell Genedlaethol Cymru
The National Library of Wales

Noddir gan
Lywodraeth
Cynulliad Cymru
Sponsored by
Welsh Assembly
Government

Printing: Cambrian Printers
Published by The National Library of Wales
First published April 2007

Contents

PART 2

Foreword

The National Library of Wales was established by Royal Charter in 1907. It collects, preserves and maintains manuscript and printed matter, maps, photographs, visual and audio-visual and electronic material relating to the people of Wales and the Celtic peoples and similar material which furthers the aims of education and literary and scientific research. As a legal deposit library it has the right to claim a copy of every printed work published in Britain and Ireland. Supported by the National Assembly for Wales, it is the primary research library and archive in Wales and has a recognized standing among other research libraries in the United Kingdom and beyond. From its majestic position overlooking Cardigan Bay, it has established itself as one of the great libraries of the world.

Its particular credential, naturally, is as custodian of the history and mind of Wales. Its collections, in various forms, encapsulate the ups-and-downs of the Welsh experience.

In this book Trevor Fishlock crystallizes those changes in a succinct and brilliant essay followed by appropriate selective illustrative panels accompanied by telling commentary. He views Wales from the touch-line and with his vast experience as a premier journalist who has reported from – and on – most regions of the world. From his *Wales and the Welsh* of 1972, Trevor Fishlock has been a discerning reporter and television observer of the Welsh scene: even as a roving foreign correspondent he kept an eye on the fortunes and misfortunes of his grandmotherland. He knows the sinews of our people and the hills and crannies of our countryside. The result is a narrative of exquisite clarity and elegance providing a splendid commentary on a representative miscellany of our collections at The National Library of Wales.

R Brinley Jones
President

March 2007

Supplementary Charter,

...tes. of the Court of

...ssed by a majority

...eeting of the Court,

...ding at an ordinary

...e than two years

...ncil, a certificate

...dorsed on the

...be sufficient

also any of the Articles...
may be repealed, varie...
Governors of the Libra...

2. A Special Statu...
of two-thirds of the Me...
confirmed by a similar...
meeting of the Court...
later and submitted t...

(3) Words importing...
gender.

In witness whereof We have caused these Our Letters to be made Patent.

Witness Ourself at Westminster the *nineteenth* day of *March* in the *seventh* year of Our Reign.

By Warrant under The King's Sign Manual. *Muir Mackenzie*

Preface

The National Library of Wales is many things, but probably for most people it is a multifaceted mirror of the life of Wales down the ages.

For 100 years our systematic aim has been to assemble, safeguard and give public access to the documentary record of Wales and the Welsh. The result is a rich mix of media, of periods and of voices. Whatever the subject – the earliest Welsh poetry, the Rebecca Riots, boxing heroes of the 1930s or the music of the Manic Street Preachers – the streams of the National Library's collections flow together to form an inexhaustible reservoir of knowledge and imagination.

It matters little with what motivation our users approach the collections: in a spirit of rigorous academic research, to extend knowledge or learn new skills, or out of simple curiosity. Nowadays it matters much less *how* they make their approach: through a visit to Aberystwyth, through exhibitions, talks or educational events in other places,

or through the internet. What is important is that all of them feel that they can take advantage of what we hold in trust for them.

One of our constant tasks in The National Library of Wales has been to draw attention to the potential contained within the collections. Though we have turned increasingly in recent years to electronic means of achieving this aim, there is still a critical role for one of humanity's most ingenious and lasting inventions, and the original random access memory device, the printed book. Hence this handsome volume by Trevor Fishlock.

Like a skilled angler Trevor has cast his line repeatedly into the waters of the National Library and has brought to the bank a glittering catch of Welsh fish. Some will be familiar, others more exotic, but all of them have a story to tell about Wales and its history. And unlike most reservoirs this one is very unlikely to be over-fished to exhaustion. The Library's collections await many more explorers, today and, we hope, for centuries to come.

Andrew M.W. Green
Librarian

March 2007

1. Mountain majesty:
Llyn Cau, Cadair Idris.
Kyffin Williams, c.1950

The Quest

Anation is a narrative, a people's adventure in time. The story of Wales spans sixteen hundred years and its chief wonder is the survival of the Welsh. The twists and attritions of history often threatened to make rubble of the people's hopes that their country would survive as a distinct place with a distinctive voice. But endure it has. One meaning of the word Wales is tenacity.

For many years the Welsh feared that conquest and assimilation would reduce their story to a footnote in the annals of Britain, with a beginning, a middle and an arid end. But through the canyons of the centuries sturdy spirits carried a flame and promised that however precarious the path, Wales would live and the Welsh people would speak for it.

It was never easy. In wintry times hearts ached and hopes shrivelled. Wales was often deserted by its governing caste and disdained as poor and remote, 'a Country,' it was said in the seventeenth century, 'in the World's back-side.'

For all that, a sinewy resilience prevailed. Like the Snowdon lily, bright and brave in wind-torn rocks, the idea of Wales bloomed in adversity. Poets and scholars had their uses, summoning myths and heroes to create a past both inspiring and validating, darning history's holes with legends. Like friendship and marriage, belief always needed constant repair.

The tradition of a linguistic and literary continuity stretching arterially from the sixth century has been one of the two forces in the shaping of modern Wales. The other was the evolution of the plural civilization of the southern valleys in the great industrial accelerando of the nineteenth and twentieth centuries.

During the seismic heaves of the Victorian age a renascent national consciousness in Wales called for unifying institutions to assert and encourage Welsh aspirations and make bridges into the future. The first of these, the University of Wales, had its romantic and penurious beginnings in 1872. Miners' pennies, those small and poignant emblems, helped to make a reality of the dream.

One of the University's compelling purposes was to create an educated leadership from the ranks of the ordinary people. When it received its charter in 1893 it stood as a striking expression of national feeling and a mark of achievement and self-respect. Meanwhile, the National Eisteddfod, with its unique ornament of bardic ritual, took root as a significant influence in music and literature.

Both the National Library and National Museum originated in the same patriotic impulse of the times and embraced their roles as dynamic witnesses of the Welsh experience, storehouses of loved treasures, the places of palpable proof. With the university they formed a permanent expedition to explore the country's history and culture. A scholarly wind began to blow, winnowing the myths, finding and affirming the realities of the nation.

The National Library was established by a royal charter in 1907 and rose like a keep on the western slope of Penglais Hill above Aberystwyth, a landmark facing the curve of Cardigan Bay. It took almost half a century to complete the main building. The eye is drawn to its sentinel grandeur.

It, too, began life with the help of working men's pennies and evolved in stature and affection as the nation's library, the living memory of the people. It works and grows as the embodiment of a pledge, a determination that the epic of Wales and its meanings will never be lost. In the twenty-first century its energy springs both from its long reach into the past and its expanding role in a quest, the discovery of a history far more rich and illuminating than had ever been imagined.

The Western peninsula

It has been aptly said that Wales is a country of about the right size for one person to know reasonably well in one lifetime. The land itself is an eloquent narrator. Walk to any of the high places and much of the story lies within your gaze.

This is a maritime country and no place in it is very far from the sea. Snowdon itself is a resort of cackling gulls. From your salient you may glimpse distant promontories, or ships in the haze, or ports as snug as snooker pockets. The waves surge and fall on a long lee shore where Atlantic gales schooled generations of schoonermen and famous clans of coxswains. In harbour streets the houses built by captains for their dotage bear the names of ships that rolled around Cape Horn. Along the hill-slopes above the shores relentless westerlies bend the cringing trees and tilt the farmers into Kyffin poses.

2. Farmers on the Glyder Fach. Kyffin Williams

Opposite:
4. Coastal trader unloads cargo onto horse cart at New Quay, c.1905

3. Romance of sea and sky: Inner Sound, the Mumbles. James Harris

5. From the earliest days of tourism
the waterfalls of Wales have been
an unfailing attraction. Rheidol falls.
Welsh primitive, 1830–53

In many accounts of Wales the mountains make the frontispiece of the story, so rugged and resistant and so difficult of access that for centuries visitors complained of the country's remoteness. Some grumble still. The shivering Romans conquered the country only partly. Even the ruthless Normans and their successors took more than 200 years to screw it down with castles. Rain seemed so often an ally of Wales that its leaders were reputed to command the clouds. Storms wrecked Henry II's invading army in the Berwyn mountains in 1165. Knowing the bite of a Welsh winter the Black Prince gave his west-bound envoys an allowance for warm coats. Henry IV's troops fled back across the Severn in 1402, half-drowned by biblical deluge.

The first venturesome English tourists found the mountains a horror story of forbidding crags and abysses. But towards the end of the eighteenth century fashions changed and English romantics came to view the once-monstrous peaks as raw beauty in the wilderness. Guides led their guests to the new picturesque Wales of noble pinnacles and thrilling waterfalls, of exotic ferns and the legendary caves where, yes, madam, this is where King Arthur dozed.

PISTYLL RHAIADR.

6. 'The finest fall of water my eyes
ever beheld,' said an early tourist:
Pistyll Rhaiadr. J. Green, 1794.
After John Evans

Everywhere in Wales the buildings and ruined walls have much to teach. Summer bees in fallen abbeys suggest the murmur of prayer, of medieval scholarship and the scratch of the scriptorium. Time may have softened the castles' menace and the sinister aspect of their silhouettes; yet they remain both powerful images of conquest and of the sturdy defiance they were made to crush.

Across the country the names of churches and villages and towns speak of a loyalty to the memories of those wandering holy men,

David, Teilo, Cadog, Dyfrig, Beuno and others, who sowed the seed of Wales's early Christian character. We know little of them, save for a few fantastic stories. Yet six centuries after his death the still-luminous fame of David the water-drinker won him the status of patron saint. Around 600 parishes, covering more than half the 8,000 square mile territory of Wales, have the place-name prefix of llan. It signifies an enclosure that was originally a sanctified burial place.

7. Stones steeped in prayer: Llanthony Abbey from the North side. Revd John Parker, 29 August 1843

Wall of S clerestory fell 5 yrs ago in the afternoon of Ash Wednesday after a thaw and with a violent wind it fell to the South & several pillars fell with it.

W S Landor owner of Llantony by purchase from Col Wood who had it from Lord Oxford's family

old men remember tower 37 feet higher than now.

Llantony, from the North side. August 29. 1843.

In the hills farmhouses white and grey bear witness to centuries of hard labour on rough grazing. Mansions, parkland and avenues of trees tell of magisterial rule and great estates. Mountainsides, moors and upland scree are sectored by drystone walls and also by fences of slate shards, blue and green.

Long before French monks planted the eternal sheep on the hills, Wales was a cattle country. In colourful spectacle drovers and cowboys urged their unruly black herds to London and to final glory as the roast beef of old England. As carriers of money the cattle bosses were also pioneer bankers and the conduits of information. The snaking trails they made across Wales can still be traced and walked. You can follow them down the valleys and over river fords, past baleful battlements, around churches and gaunt chapels and into the yards of the Drovers Arms.

In more than four centuries of to and fro, from Welsh hills to English markets, the drovers saw the story unfold, the monasteries looted, the grand houses constructed, the smoke and spark of the first smelters and forges, the early nonconformist outposts, the bridges, canals, stagecoach roads, turnpikes and white milestones. In the end they watched the relentless navvy armies building the railways that did away with the droving life.

They saw the infancy of the age in which furnace fire rouged the sky and the land was gouged for iron, copper and lead, the forests felled and whole hills flensed for slate. They saw the early migrations and watched the people tramping from the farms to labour in the volcanic towns of the new Wales. After iron there was coal, its epoch lasting roughly a century and a quarter, its zenith from 1870 to 1914. Turned inside out the landscape became the greatest source of energy on earth, and the name of Cardiff became a virtual synonym for coal.

8. A plas in the sun: Gwaenynog Hall, Denbigh, painted for Thomas Pennant by John Ingleby, 1796

9. Sheep pound: a note issued by a drovers' bank

10. Dolbadarn castle, thirteenth-century
residence of the princes of Gwynedd
overlooking Llyn Padarn, Llanberis.
T. Catherall, 1852

11. Colliery rescue in south Wales:
A Perilous Passage.
Herbert Johnson, 1875

12. 'Deep in sunless pits' wrote poet W.H. Davies.
Miners photographed in the Rhondda

We live today in the aftermath of that tumult and all it meant. So much vividness and clamour vanished so suddenly; and then a certain silence ensued, like the quiet after a storm at sea.

In expiation and renewal the people planted the wounded hills and filled the dark craters of the no-man's-lands. They rinsed the scungy rivers and made them silvery for salmon, sculpted parks and laid woodland pathways, heritage trails in the jargon. They set up plaques explaining what had happened here, so that a new generation could look around and try to imagine the smoke, the uproar and stupendous human endeavour; and hardly believe it.

13. A sinew of empire: Cardiff docks in the 1890s. A. Duncan, L. Godfrey

14. Sylvan smoke: Coal works, a view near Neath. John Hassell, 1798

Drawn & Engraved by J.Hassell.

COAL WORKS.

A View near Neath in Glamorganshire, South Wales.

Between three & five west

The country and people of Wales began to emerge in the fifth century as the Romans gradually ended their 400 years of occupation in Britain. We know little about the origins of the migrants who peopled the British islands before the Roman conquest. Over many centuries offshoots of the tribes wandering over southern and south-western Europe made their way to Britain. After the Roman withdrawal small groups of Scandinavians and of Germanic tribes, Angles, Saxons, Jutes and others, began to spread slowly through Britain. Out of this process grew a myth that Anglo-Saxons exterminated the indigenous people and

15. Rockfist:
Harlech castle.
Henry Gastineau, c.1830

drove the remnants westward. In reality the newcomers assimilated and integrated with the existing inhabitants and with them laid the foundations of what would become England. They were pagan. In the land of Wales the small cult of Christianity, which spread during the sixth century, helped to sharpen a Welsh difference.

The Brittonic language evolved into Welsh; and stanzas penned late in the sixth century by the founding poets Aneirin and Taliesin sing to us from that early dawn. The people began to call themselves Cymry, meaning fellow-countrymen, or comrades. Their neighbours used Saxon words, Wales and Welsh, to describe the country and a particular people different from themselves. In the eighth century, Offa of Mercia marked his kingdom's western boundary with an earth and stone embankment stretching 160 miles between Chepstow and Prestatyn. He thereby defined an eastern margin of Wales and helped to propagate an idea of Welsh identity.

This dyke is a reality we can cling to, a handrail, as we look into those early centuries and the patchwork of warring Welsh kingdoms whose rough and tumble fortunes were carved by dynasties and ever-bloody swords. Through the mists of the ninth century strides battling Rhodri Mawr, his name still renowned. Through inheritance and shrewd marriage he united the kingdoms of Gwynedd, Powys, and Seisyllwg in the south-west. He resolutely confronted the Scandinavian invaders, those incessant pillagers and slave-hunters who terrified the coastal settlements, and finally met his desired warrior's death fighting Anglo-Saxon forces in 877.

His grandson's name also resonates. Hywel Dda, Hywel the Good, ruled much of Wales and may have helped to compile some of the tenth-century body of law that bears his name. Among its other qualities this legal code was a work of serious purpose, a badge of nationhood and unity. It enshrined a simple justice, set out the values of pigs and people, and described the proper tributes due to a king. It remained a useful legal guidance in parts of Wales until superseded by the Tudor laws 600 years later.

Early in the tenth century the pugnacious and ever-adaptable Viking raiders settled in northern France and created their colony of Normandy. They became the dominant military force of Europe. Duke William of Normandy sailed to England in October 1066, crushed Harold's army at Hastings and took the throne. Within four years he held all England in his grasp and replaced English by French as the language of law. The Normans looked down their armoured noses at the defeated English. When they raised their eyes to the west they saw a country led by unruly princes, ripe for beating into subservience.

To deal with the problem of the Welsh William established a land barrier between Wales and England, a border territory called the March, from the French word for frontier. He created earldoms based on the strategic

towns of Hereford, Shrewsbury and Chester. The Marcher lords, the earls and their subaltern barons, were ruthless men of war who ruled as virtual monarchs in their realms and became landowners by right of conquest.

Their mounted and armoured knights were as fearsome as twentieth-century tanks. Pushing westward they easily seized the ripe lands in the river valleys and coastal plains and raised 600 timber forts on earth mounds to command key roads and river crossings. Their men could build such forts in eight days. Once a district was subdued they consolidated their grip with intimidating stone ramparts and made southern Wales the most castled part of Britain.

Their advance faltered at the end of the eleventh century when the Welsh rose in opposition and forced them to accept the rule of native princes in Gwynedd, Powys, Ceredigion and what would later be Carmarthenshire. In conquered districts, however, small colonial towns grew under the protection of the castles, English traders settled, French and English speech took root. In parts of Pembrokeshire and Gower substantial numbers of Flemish colonists shouldered the Welsh aside. The twelfth century in Wales was a time of transition and acute crisis as the Normans pressed hard for mastery. A realization grew among people in the varied jigsaw pieces of Wales that they shared an identity marking them out from their neighbours in England.

More than sixty years after William's

16. Against the law: the crime of hair-pulling depicted in the Laws of Hywel Dda

17. Hunting law according to Hywel

conquest, the new regime determined on a spiritual occupation of Wales to reinforce their military hold. To the Normans the Welsh church looked disorganized. It lacked a strong ecclesiastical grip, had no backbone of monasteries and priestly hierarchy, no imposing stone churches, no Welsh saints worth honouring. Many of the clergy were married, not celibate. The new authorities saw sense in bringing the Welsh church into their control. They obliged the Welsh bishops to kneel to the king and the archbishop of Canterbury; and thereby ended Wales's isolation from European Christendom.

The conquerors also shipped French monks to Wales to build monasteries and enforce the integration. As it happened, the Benedictines were too Norman in outlook and too close to the castle walls to reach out to the Welsh. Many of the white-robed Cistercians, on the other hand, endeared themselves to the people. They raised thirteen graceful abbeys which became popular places of pilgrimage, the first at Tintern beside the Wye in 1131. They also spread their knowledge of agriculture,

ploughed the land, built roads and small ships and smelted iron. They grew friendly with princely rulers and interested in the native literature. Their austerity and fondness for manual work seemed to the Welsh an echo of the legendary ideals of Saint David. Although the conquerors sought to replace Welsh holy men with their own saints, the people resisted and remained loyal to Saint David and his brothers.

19. Princes' perch: Dolbadarn castle on a rock at the end of Llanberis Pass, built for the thirteenth-century princes of Gwynedd. Here Llywelyn the Great imprisoned his brother for twenty-three years and Owain Glyn Dŵr held Lord Grey of Ruthin for ransom.
J.M.W. Turner, c.1799

18. Power point: Conwy castle. William Daniell, 1813

View of Conway Castle Caernarvonshire.

The Manacle towers

In the thirteenth century Welsh hopes of an existence independent of the power of England lay with two forward-thinking princes of Gwynedd. Llywelyn the Great, 1173–1240, the outstanding ruler of medieval Wales, was confident enough to act decisively when he found the leading Marcher lord being too intimate with his wife: he hanged him. Llywelyn's grandson, Llywelyn ap Gruffudd, 1225–82, seemed set fair to rule a united country as prince of Wales. The vessel of his hopes struck the unyielding rock of Edward I, the strongest of England's medieval kings.

20. Battle cries: the horror of face-to face medieval warfare

Edward's iron purpose was to bring Wales and Scotland under his overlordship. Llywelyn antagonized him in 1276 by failing to show a proper deference and refusing to pay a financial tribute. Edward branded him a rebel and marched on Wales to bloody his nose. He seized Llywelyn's lands and confined him to the stretch of Gwynedd west of the Conwy, an action that rendered the title of prince of Wales derisory.

In 1282, that fateful year, Edward invaded Wales again. This time he marched to crush a revolt led by Llywelyn's brother, Dafydd. Llywelyn himself had little choice but to join the rising and was killed by an English soldier in a skirmish near Builth on 11 December. He was fifty-seven. His head was carried to London where, blackened and impaled on a spike, it served as a grisly punctuation marking the end of independent Wales. Edward sent a message to the Pope in Rome saying that Wales was finished. In 1283 Dafydd was captured and eviscerated alive at Shrewsbury. To many in Wales it really did seem like the end of the world. 'O God,' cried an anguished poet, 'that the sea might engulf the land.'

The king built a ring of forbidding castles to secure his conquest, stone fists in the Welsh face. The walls of Flint, Rhuddlan, Builth and Aberystwyth rose after the war of 1277; Conwy, Caernarfon and Harlech after the crushing of Llywelyn; and handsome Beaumaris after a fierce rebellion in 1294. The building director of these masterpieces, James of Saint George, from Savoy in the French Alps, was an authority on the construction of forts in the Middle East and Turkey. The ramparts of Constantinople inspired the imperial magnificence of Caernarfon, the greatest fort and icon of Edward's conquest.

21. A time of grief: the Chronicle of the Princes recorded the death of Llywelyn, 'the last prince'

22. The stamp of conquest: Caernarfon castle. Moses Griffith

As Master of the King's Works in Wales, James called up armies of English carpenters, masons, smiths, plumbers, carters and ditch diggers who walked to a gathering point at Chester whence they were despatched to Wales. Stone, timber, iron, rope and nails arrived by ship from Bristol and Liverpool. During the building season from April to November around 4,000 men toiled for seven days a week on several castles at once. They built Conwy quickly, in five seasons. At Caernarfon a smith thoughtfully placed iron spikes on the head of a statue of the king to deter mannerless birds. Five centuries later the writer Thomas Pennant described Edward's castles as 'the badges of our subjection.' They also stood as tributes to the people's resistance.

In 1296 Master James asked the exchequer to send more cash for building works and warned of Welsh fury. 'As you well know,' he wrote, 'Welshmen are Welshmen and if there is war with France and Scotland we shall need to watch them all the more closely. Sirs, for God's sake be quick with the money.'

War in Wales emptied the king's coffers. He spent £80,000 on the castles and three times as much on his campaigns to bring the Welsh to heel and was forced to borrow prodigiously from Italian bankers. Thus huge spending in Wales undermined his plan to subjugate Scotland and create a monolithic Britain.

When Edward conquered Wales the country's population was a quarter of a million, a twelfth of what it is today.

Mostly the people lived not in villages but in homesteads or, here and there, in hamlets encircling a church. As frugal as monks, they existed chiefly on oatmeal, cheese, butter and meat. In spring many of them moved with their animals to the hafod, the summer home on the hill, and descended in autumn to the hendre, the main homestead in the valley.

English traders and officials made their homes within the protective shield of the castles, privileged colonists who scorned the second-class Welsh scattered beyond the gates. Conquest made all of Wales a Marcher lordship and the crestfallen people had to make the best of it, demonized and forbidden to bear arms, to buy land or conduct business and, in some places, to brew ale. Excluded in their own country, Welshmen only rarely secured official positions.

It was easy, however, for Welsh soldiers to find work. They were formidable archers. Years of fighting had made Wales, as R.S. Thomas put it, 'taut for war', and many young men escaped oppression by enlisting as mercenaries in the English armies in campaigns in Scotland and France. They saw something of other lands and their pay contributed significantly to the economy at home. Six thousand Welsh soldiers, bright in green and white clothing, helped the Black Prince defeat the French at Crécy in 1346, the first battle won by arrows rather than by close-quarters fighting with swords.

The Black Death, history's worst disease-disaster, a combination of rat-borne plague and perhaps anthrax, killed a third of Europe's population in 1348-49. It scythed more than a quarter of the people of Wales. Perhaps Dafydd ap Gwilym, the sunny prince of Welsh poets, fell to its horrific virulence.

It struck four more times in the fourteenth century, compounding the wretchedness made by famine. Landowners pressed survivors of the plague to pay ever larger taxes and seized their land when they failed to do so.

Grievances against avaricious rulers, against humiliations and 'the sting of English law', grew into a rumbling thunder. In September 1400 the storm burst at last in the revolt of Owain Glyn Dŵr.

23. Stronghold: a photograph, c.1860, captures the drama of Harlech. Owain Glyn Dŵr besieged the castle in 1404, made it his capital and held a parliament here. English forces seized it in 1409 and took Owain's wife and children prisoner

Meteor
of a
troubled heaven

No war in Wales wrought so much ruin. Across the land smoke drifted from burning towns. The dead lay in the embers. The living fled. The hungry straggled over unsown fields and bloodied streams. Soldiers destroyed mills and manors.

The fighting raged across the early years of the fifteenth century, a furious shove against what Owain Glyn Dŵr called the slavery imposed by the English. Hailed as prince of Wales, he drew support from many Welsh squires and also from the peasantry, the clergy and numerous Welsh students at Oxford who travelled to join his cause. From 1402 to 1404 he blazed as a military comet. He fought mostly as a guerrilla leader, conducting a war of ambushes and raids, his men moving rapidly along the mountain paths they knew

so well; but he also led large forces with success. He steadily won authority in much of Wales, invaded Glamorgan and Gwent and took control of large stretches of territory in the lowlands. He attacked Caernarfon and Cydweli and seized the castles at Aberystwyth and Harlech.

At the height of his campaigning, in 1404, he called parliaments at Machynlleth and Harlech and set out his plans for two universities and an independent church, institutions that would nourish a Welsh state. He formed an alliance with France and made an agreement with the Percy and Mortimer families of England to share territory. This provided that, had he been victorious, some of the English borderland would have been joined to Wales.

24. Cavalcade:
Owain Glyn Dŵr on the
march, as imagined by artist
Margaret Jones, 2000

25. 'At my birth/ The front of heaven was full of fiery shapes.' Owain Glyn Dŵr, the hero on his charger, portrayed by A. C. Michael in 1915

After four years of war the English hold on Wales was tenuous. Glyn Dŵr seemed in all ways the liberator promised in ancient prophecies. These gave him some comfort and inspiration. But his tide began to ebb. In the early years of the war Henry IV was short of money. In 1404 he passed the fighting command in Wales to his son, later Henry V, who had a military skill beyond his eighteen years. With more money to draw on, the young prince ground away at Wales and steadily his superior resources sapped Glyn Dŵr's strength. Welsh hopes leaked away. By 1410 Glyn Dŵr was a fugitive and by 1414 the last Welsh revolt was over.

In his defeat of Glyn Dŵr, Henry V achieved another conquest of Wales. He restored English authority and strengthened the castles. He was not especially vengeful but he made disillusioned Wales pay a price. Men who had fought for Glyn Dŵr knelt in their hundreds and swore loyalty to the king. English officials sold pardons to former combatants for immense and ruinous sums. They also renewed the old sanctions and extortions, the second-class citizenship, the slights and acrimony that had fed Welsh grievances in the years before the war.

Our man *in* London

Sixty years after the Glyn Dŵr storm abated a turn in the fortunes of the Anglesey Tudor family persuaded the bards to polish their prophecies once more. The Tudors had supported Glyn Dŵr and one of them, Rhys, was executed for doing so. His son Owain, however, found a position in the household of Henry V. In 1422 he secretly married the king's widow Catherine of Valois, daughter of the French king and mother of Henry VI. Owain fought in the Wars of the Roses, the thirty years of struggle for the English crown between Lancastrian and Yorkist families. Yorkists executed him at Hereford in 1461.

His grandson, Henry Tudor, born to the thirteen-year-old heiress Margaret Beaufort in 1457, was imprisoned in Raglan castle from 1461 to 1470. In 1471, his life threatened by Yorkists, he fled from Pembroke to Brittany. Jasper Tudor, earl of Pembroke, his uncle and guardian, accompanied him.

During fourteen years of exile Jasper schemed to make his nephew king of England.

26. From here to the throne, Henry Tudor's birthplace: Pembroke castle. Paul Sandby, 1808

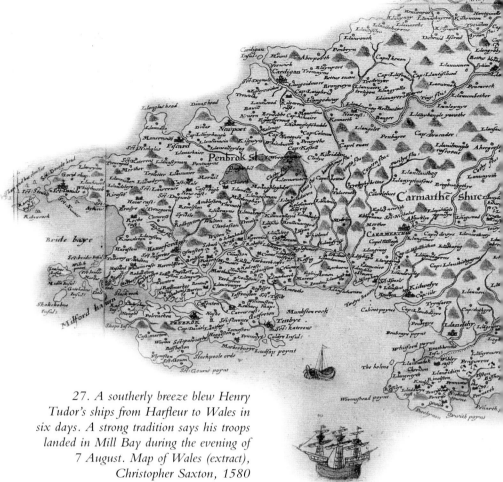

The claim was shaky but in their messianic verses the bards promised that Henry would be the new King Arthur who, as a Welshman, and therefore, in Welsh eyes, a true Briton, would regain the ancient British throne. Henry in fact was half-English and a quarter-French. But he was also a quarter-Welsh, had been born in Pembroke castle and claimed descent from Cadwaladr, a seventh-century British king.

It was enough. In August 1485, leading an army of 4,000 and backed by the king of France, twenty-eight-year-old Henry sailed to wrest the crown from Richard III. He landed near Dale in Milford Haven and marched by way of Llanbadarn, Machynlleth and Mathafarn to the Long Mountain near Welshpool.

The hill slope here remains evocative: imagination conjures Henry's rendezvous with Welsh chiefs, including Rhys ap Thomas of Dynefwr, who risked everything to join him. He crossed into England and fifteen days after landing defeated Richard III at Bosworth in Leicestershire. He fought under a twenty-seven-foot banner bearing Cadwaladr's red dragon emblem on a green and white background. In time this would become the national flag of Wales. As Henry VII, the last man to win the throne of England by the sword, he founded the Tudor royal dynasty which endured for more than a century.

Wales hailed 'the son of prophecy' and enjoyed the spectacle of the English crown

27. A southerly breeze blew Henry Tudor's ships from Harfleur to Wales in six days. A strong tradition says his troops landed in Mill Bay during the evening of 7 August. Map of Wales (extract), Christopher Saxton, 1580

glinting on a Welsh head. Henry knew the value of posing as a Welsh hero and called his first son Arthur. He served the myth, and the myth served him. Welsh loyalty was important to his security. He rewarded his supporters with jobs at court, made his Welsh Bosworth veterans his Yeomen of the Guard and appointed his uncle Jasper to manage Wales and the March. Thanks to the Bosworth effect Welshmen became sheriffs and bishops for the first time in the fifteenth century.

Nevertheless Henry knew that favouritism fathered resentment and shrewdly reined what love he had for the land of his birth. He ruled for twenty-four years and never saw Wales again. But his presence in London made the city more attractive to Welshmen, forerunners of a professional class of lawyers and businessmen who lived by their wits, of scholars, physicians and civil servants, all of them able to work in English.

Henry's gift to the people of England and Wales was political stability after years of wearying and bloody dispute over succession. His second son Henry VIII, Prince Arthur having died, occupied a secure throne and established centralized rule in a united kingdom. Legislation of 1536 and 1543 incorporated Wales into England and was the heart of Henry VIII's policy in Wales. Framed by the king's masterminding secretary Thomas Cromwell it brought the Welsh in from the cold, awarding them equal citizenship with Englishmen, twenty-seven seats in parliament and the right to inherit land. Essentially the new laws consolidated English authority and confirmed the fact of union set out in the Statute of Rhuddlan in 1284. At that time the shires of Carmarthen, Cardigan, Merioneth, Anglesey, Caernarfon and Flint were created. Henry VIII's reforms of 1536 at last ended the anomalous Marcher lordships, those troublesome remnants of the Norman conquest, and these were redrawn as the shires of Monmouth, Brecon, Radnor, Montgomery, Denbigh, Glamorgan and Pembroke.

For uniformity's sake the Tudor settlement

28. Tremble and obey: Henry VIII's portrait on a Great Sessions Breconshire plea roll, 1542

designated English as the sole language of the courts and administration in Wales. No monoglot Welsh-speaker could hold a public office. A system of cheap and accessible justice, the Courts of Great Sessions, was set up; and it would last until 1830. Welsh landowners were given a primary role in running Wales. Appointed as justices, they were 'magistrates of their own nation.' Meanwhile, many gentlemen hastened from Wales to prosper in London's commerce.

This suited Henry. He wanted Wales contented. During the 1530s he and Cromwell engineered religious Reformation, ending papal authority in England and Wales and splitting European Christianity. There was an obsessive concern that Catholic Spain and France might attempt invasion through Wales to reverse Henry's reforms. Meanwhile, desperate for funds, Henry abolished the monasteries, forty-seven of them in Wales, some of them centres of Welsh learning, and seized their wealth. Ransacked for their lead, glass, stone and treasures, religious buildings slipped into ruin. The monasteries' age of glory and leadership was in any case in decline. Under the eyes of an indifferent people, the gentry swooped like buzzards and bought up the abbey acres to enlarge their estates, while many monks quit the cloisters to scratch new livings as parish priests.

29. Stronghold of the Marcher lords: Abergavenny castle, S. Sparrow, 1784

30. Prince's cradle: Dolwyddelan castle was reputedly the birthplace in 1173 of Llywelyn the Great. Samuel and Nathaniel Buck, 1743

31. William Morgan by Keith Bowen, 1988. A postage stamp design marking the 400th anniversary of Morgan's Bible

32. Anchoring Wales: Saint Matthew's gospel from the 1588 Bible

Words
for all

The invention of printing was one of history's great revolutionary beginnings with fundamental long-term consequences. Around 1453 Johannes Gutenberg, a goldsmith at Mainz in Germany, built a press with movable type made from lead and tin. He published the first printed book, a Latin Bible, in 1455–56. Before the birth of printing scribes, working in the traditional way with pen and ink took more than a year and half to copy a Bible. Gutenberg's press printed hundreds of volumes in that time, and much more cheaply.

Printing spread rapidly to Rome, Milan, Naples, Paris, Lyon and Valencia. Music was printed in 1473. The first books in English, a history of Troy and a guide to chess, were printed in Bruges by the translator William Caxton. He established the first press in London in 1476 and printed around ninety books, more than seventy of them in English, including works by Geoffrey Chaucer and Sir Thomas Malory's popular working of the Arthurian legends, Morte d'Arthur.

Within fifty years of the publication of the pioneering Bible Europe's printers expanded the universe of the human mind with 40,000 titles and up to twenty million books. Henry VIII owned a library of 1,000 volumes and scribbled his comments in the margins of some of them.

Printing was part of the fuel and fire of the Renaissance and of the Reformation. The Catholic church could do little to halt the flow of the printed word. Protestant pressure for an English Bible and English services threatened the authority of the Latin-based church and its priestly monopoly of knowledge. In the 1520s the preacher William Tyndale answered the call for an English Bible, working in Germany because it was too dangerous to make a translation at home. Copies he sent to England were burnt by bishops; and Tyndale himself was condemned for heresy and burnt at the stake in Antwerp in 1536. The simple sentences of his translation decisively influenced the development of English. Thomas Cranmer's masterpiece rendering of the Book of Common Prayer was similarly mellifluous. Shakespeare's plays and poetry demonstrated how glorious the language could be.

The implications of printing's power to move minds was not lost on Welsh scholars. They began to fear that if their native language were not dignified by print it would rot. They argued that the lack of a Welsh Bible threatened the progress of the Reformation. Few of the ordinary people in Wales knew English and, denied the word of God, were heading for dangerous ignorance.

In any case, church reform was depriving them of the routines of religion to which they were accustomed. In 1563 the Denbighshire lawyer William Salesbury and his friends supported a private Act of Parliament commanding the bishops of Wales and Hereford, a county where many Welsh-speakers lived, to publish the Bible and Prayer Book in Welsh. Queen Elizabeth's consent reflected an anxiety that in the vicious Catholic-Protestant struggle Catholic intriguers might gain a foothold in Wales. Welsh Bibles would be bricks in the defensive wall.

But Salesbury's pedantic and eccentric translation of the New Testament, published in 1567, was difficult to read and, when read aloud, tormented the ear. In 1578 William Morgan, vicar of Llanrhaeadr-ym-Mochnant, began his masterly translation of the complete Bible which was published in 1588. Bishops were ordered, on pain of a fine of forty pounds, to place the Welsh and English versions side by side in church so that 'by conferring both tongues together' the Welsh would readily learn English.

It did not work out like that. Morgan's Bible anchored Wales to the Protestant faith but it also became the chariot of Welsh culture. The literary genius of Wales had flowered for many years mostly in poetry. Reaching out to the people, Morgan wrote in the rhythms of the spoken language and created a new and accessible prose, enchanting readers and listeners with the beauty and possibilities of their own tongue.

This translation was the foundation of all the Welsh prose that followed. The pocket edition, Y Beibl Bach, first published 1630, entered thousands of homes. William Morgan's Bible influenced the way the language was used and in time helped to define his country. The people spoke Welsh and in a particular way spoke Morgan.

33. Country life:
Baptism at Llanbadarn Fawr.
Welsh primitive, c.1840

Land
&lord

Landowners in Wales prospered in the times of Elizabeth and her successor James I, during the years from 1558 to 1625. Some struck it rich in lead and coal mining, some in foreign trade as America and the East were opened up. Thomas Myddleton, a founding merchant of the East India Company, bought the lordship of Chirk and became lord mayor of London in 1613. Richard Clough of Denbigh made a fortune in Antwerp and was the second of the four husbands of Catrin of Berain whose flock of children figured so prominently among the squirearchy that she was known as the 'Mother of Wales.'

Through their dynastic marriages the landowners combined their acres in large estates so that the ownership of much of Wales devolved to a small elite. The mansion families also carved up parliamentary representation between them for the next two centuries. Many of them, magnates and minor gentry alike, looked east to England, grew more anglicized, took English wives and invited Englishmen to marry their daughters. They schooled their sons in England or in the Tudor grammar schools like those at Abergavenny, Brecon, Carmarthen, Cowbridge and Ruthin where no Welsh was taught. In culture, manners and religion, and as allies of the English establishment, they grew increasingly distant from their own people.

During the Civil War of the seventeenth century they mostly remained loyal to Charles I in his struggle against parliament; but not deeply so. Fearing for their estates they usually kept their heads down. Wales interested the king as a supply base, a refuge across the Severn, a link to Ireland and a source of cash and conscripts. Hundreds of Welshmen, however, resisted enlistment. At a time of plagues and poor harvests life was hard enough without the demands of military service.

A few Welsh squires supported parliament. Thomas Myddleton, lord of Chirk, whose father had been mayor of London, captured Montgomery castle from the royalists in 1643. But in general the gentry breathed uneasily during Oliver Cromwell's puritan rule as Lord Protector in the 1650s. They were mightily relieved when the crown was restored in 1660. That same Thomas Myddleton who had seized Montgomery and enthusiastically drove royalist clergy from their churches tired

of Cromwell. He was elected to the parliament which paved the way to the restoration of Charles II.

Most of Wales worshipped in the Anglican churches. There were few Catholics and extreme puritans. A census in 1676 counted 153,000 Anglicans in Wales, 4,000 dissenters and only 1,000 Catholics. Inevitably, the spread of reading led to interpretations of the scriptures different from the teachings of the church. The first seeds of dissent germinated in Wales before the Civil War. In 1639 dissenters gathered at Llanfaches, Monmouthshire, to found the first nonconformist congregation in Wales. In the 1660s and 1670s the government persecuted and jailed large numbers of Quakers for their beliefs, so much so that many fled to America in 1682 and founded the colony that became Pennsylvania. Dissenters often had to meet clandestinely. One day the authorities fell on Blaencanaid farm, near Merthyr Tydfil, and took twenty-four worshippers to jail. The toleration law of 1689 allowed dissenters to meet in licensed chapels provided the doors were not locked, but forbade them to hold public office.

*34. Library house:
Peniarth, Llanegryn*

35. The first Methodist association meeting in Wales, 1743: Y Sasiwn Gyntaf, John Cennick, Joseph Humphreys, John Powell, William Williams, George Whitefield, Daniel Rowland and Howel Harris. Hugh Williams, 1912

Nevertheless, nonconformity began its dogged march. It drew strength from its preachers, determined savers of souls, and in particular from the war waged on illiteracy by Griffith Jones, vicar of Llanddowror, Carmarthenshire. From the 1730s he trained young men to travel the countryside, usually in winter when people had more time to study, teaching men, women and children, young and old, to read the Bible.

For more than thirty years his classes fed the people on words, spreading literacy through tens of thousands of farm families, encouraged religious debate and created a market for Welsh books. As a powerful preacher Griffith

Jones inspired the young evangelist exhorters Howel Harris and Daniel Rowland. With the preacher and gifted hymn-writer William Williams these ardent missionaries led the advance of Methodism from the mid-1730s. By 1750 more than 400 Methodist societies flourished in Wales.

As it gained territory, Methodism drove out or suppressed much of the old merriment, the fairs, music and maypole dancing. It frowned on the popular and boisterous games of quoits, wrestling, cockfighting and football, played on the northern side of churchyards, the least sacred part. Such recreation submitted to sober sabbath observance.

36. An exhortation of preachers

The reading movement pioneered by Griffith Jones was continued in the Sunday schools founded by Thomas Charles of Bala in 1789. He took the defining revolutionary step of 1811, leading the reluctant Methodist secession from the Anglican church.

Thereafter, as a new nonconformist denomination, Methodists ordained their own clergy. Some of these matured into the charismatic preachers who propelled nonconformity in Wales towards its high tide in the nineteenth century.

City of
dreams

Like any capital London was a place of renewal and fantasy, the goal of fortune-seekers. Henry VII had opened it to Welsh traders and other adventurers. During the eighteenth century it was the place where the culture of Wales chiefly flourished: Wales itself lacked a town large enough to serve as a hothouse for writers, arguers and publishers, and had no university, library or cultural focus.

At a time when the separate history of Wales seemed to have decayed, patriotic exiles debated and wrote passionately of a luminous Welsh past. The London Welsh became a force in Welsh literature. The Honourable Society of Cymmrodorion, meaning the ancient Britons, was founded in London in 1751, and the Gwyneddigion, meaning north Walians, in 1770. Their members published periodicals and collected and copied manuscripts. Booksellers, clergymen, antiquarians and scribblers of all kinds swelled the Welsh crowds at convivial evenings of poetry and harp music in taverns and coffee houses. In one of the city's inns, wrote David Samwell in his poem The Padouca Hunt,

You'll find the room
where wordy war
Is waged by
Cambrian wits.

A leading figure of the London Welsh was the irrepressible and prolific patriot Edward Williams, alias Iolo Morganwg, the principal creator of a Wales of the imagination and an inspired fable-monger. He gave his beloved Glamorgan a starring part in the inspiring and glorious history he invented for Wales. In 1792 he staged a druidic ceremony at Primrose Hill, the small beginning of the gorsedd of bards which he later implanted into the eisteddfod. His romantic mind embraced the legend of the 'Welsh Indians', supposedly the descendants of a twelfth-century Welsh prince who discovered America. He enthusiastically supported the idea of a search for the 'lost tribe.' The mountain of manuscripts he left to the National Library, eighty years before the library was founded, intrigues history researchers to this day.

By the end of the eighteenth century the spread of education in Wales itself was eroding the cultural leadership of the London Welsh. The Cymmrodorion faded in the 1780s. Re-established in 1873 it reflected a more modern and practical Victorian view. London's Welsh lawyers and businessmen, reinforced by shopkeepers, ministers and teachers, formed a chapel-minded movement more interested in the Wales of the present and the future rather than of the past. One of their chief concerns was education and they therefore added their weight to the movement for the national university and museum and library in Wales.

37. A new note: the earliest collection of traditional Welsh airs by John Parry, the blind harpist, published in London, 1742, marks the beginning of secular music in Wales

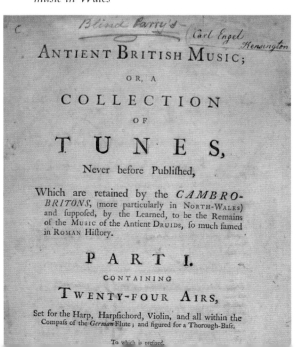

ANTIENT BRITISH MUSIC;

OR, A

COLLECTION

OF

TUNES,

Never before Publifhed,

Which are retained by the CAMBRO-BRITONS, (more particularly in NORTH-WALES) and fuppofed, by the Learned, to be the Remains of the MUSIC of the Antient DRUIDS, fo much famed in ROMAN Hiftory.

PART I.

CONTAINING

TWENTY-FOUR AIRS,

Set for the Harp, Harpfichord, Violin, and all within the Compafs of the German Flute; and figured for a Thorough-Bafs.

To which is prefixed.

Etched by Robert Cruikshank — from a memoriter drawing by E.W.

Edward Williams.

Bardd Braint a Defod.

38. 'Iolo, old Iolo,
he who knows.'
Iolo Morganwg, etching
by Robert Cruikshank:
from Recollections and
Anecdotes of Edward
Williams, Elijah Waring,
1850, frontispiece

The black domain

In the summer of 1802 Lord Nelson, with his mistress and her husband Sir William Hamilton, visited Merthyr Tydfil to see the ironworks owned by the formidable Richard Crawshay. Nelson thanked the men who forged the cannon, the Royal Navy's fearsome thunder. Crawshay's personal badge sported a pyramid of cannonballs, a nod to the source of the wealth that made him one of Britain's first millionaires. He towered in the new world of rapidly-developing technologies of fire and steam.

The wars of the eighteenth century created huge demands for guns and ammunition. Nelson, keenly aware of the debt to iron-makers, also had a seafarer's understanding of the crucial significance of Welsh copper. The Royal Navy needed a continuous supply of copper sheets to protect ships' hulls from the ravages of timber-eating teredo worms. Thomas Williams provided it. One of the greatest British magnates of the age, he owned Mynydd Parys, an Anglesey mountain almost made of copper, and ruled most of Britain's copper trade from the 1770s.

Wales grew from its underground wealth. The Romans excavated its gold, copper and silver. From medieval times landowners ran small lead and iron mines, coal pits and furnaces and by the late eighteenth century Wales was developing into a mineral-extracting and industrial country. Iron production at Bersham in Denbighshire flourished from the 1760s under John Wilkinson, maker of gun barrels and steam-engine cylinders, whose temper was as fiery as his furnaces.

Government inspectors called the eighteen miles of upland from Hirwaun to Blaenafon 'the black domain' of ironworks and collieries. It was no place for the timid. Ironmasters built on the large scale for bulk production. The monumental furnaces at Merthyr and Blaenafon seemed like temples raised to voracious gods. Their remnants still strike awe.

Carts and packhorse trains carried iron bars laboriously to the port at Cardiff until the canals built from the 1790s revolutionized the transport of heavy loads. A horse could carry 300 pounds on its back or draw 600 pounds on a cart; but it could pull twenty tons loaded on a canal barge. The rugged and twisting landscape, however, made canals difficult to engineer. More than fifty locks lay between Merthyr and Cardiff. Nevertheless, canals provided cheap transport and, looking at them today, we can only wonder at the surveying and construction skills of their builders.

In 1805 the visionary Thomas Telford fused beauty and strength in spanning the Dee valley with a high level canal aqueduct near Llangollen. He demonstrated his genius again, in 1826, with his revolutionary wrought iron suspension bridge over the Menai Strait. It set the pattern for every one of the world's suspension bridges. In 1804, only two years after Nelson was at Merthyr, Richard Trevithick built the first locomotive to run on rails. His 'portable steam engine' linked the Penydarren ironworks to the canal ten miles away. The stone blocks to which he secured his rails are still to be seen.

The Merthyr that Nelson saw was a fire mountain. The sky glowed red above the town's four gigantic ironworks, Dowlais, Cyfarthfa, Plymouth and Penydarren. Merthyr was a frontier settlement of 7,000 people, rapidly growing into the greatest iron-making centre in Britain. It remained the largest town in Wales for the next sixty years, 'a vision of Hell', according to the historian Thomas Carlyle. Housing was primitive, diseases like cholera were rife and in 1841 half the children died before the age of five. The work, whether in the ironworks or in the coal pits that fuelled them, was grinding and dangerous. Men, women and children were killed and maimed in numerous accidents. In 1830 it was common to see a hundred women queueing to fill a pail at the town's only clean well.

Yet Merthyr and her neighbouring villages were a magnet for thousands of young men from the countryside who packed their bundles and headed to the smoke to earn more than they could dream of on a hill farm. 'Dyma'r lle am arian' they wrote home. 'This is the place for money.'

By 1830 Merthyr was crowded with 30,000 people, mostly Welsh-speaking, young and radical. As well as an army of labourers there were also many skilled and proud craftsmen who sustained a lively press, pamphlets, eisteddfodau and the habit of nonconformist dissent. Here, more strongly than anywhere else, a working-class consciousness evolved, a restlessness and militancy aggravated by harsh conditions, wage cuts, high prices in the employers' truck shops where people were forced to go, the severity of debtors' courts, and anger at the lack of a working-class vote.

At the end of May 1831 the ironmaster William Crawshay cut wages at his Cyfarthfa works and 10,000 furious workers gathered in protest on a Merthyr hillside. A crowd attacked the home of a local judge and burned court records. The Merthyr rising had begun, the first violent clash in Wales between industrial workers and the ruling class. The authorities summoned troops and the crowd raised a red flag. The soldiers opened fire and killed about twenty-five people. Dic Penderyn, one of the protesters, was arrested for injuring a soldier and hanged in Cardiff. Another protester was transported to Australia.

The Reform Act in 1832, passed against a background of unrest, increased the size of the electorate by spreading the vote into the prosperous middle classes. It left much of the country under landowner rule and, by excluding industrial workers from the voting process, ensured their enduring bitterness. Truck shops, however, were made illegal. In 1839 supporters of the People's Charter, a demand for voting rights and electoral reform, rioted in the wool town of Llanidloes. In November that year thousands of Chartists,

39. Next page: Fire in the hills: South Wales industrial landscape. Penry Williams, c.1825

40. Angry years: Attack of the Chartists on the Westgate Hotel, Newport, 1839. James Flewitt Mullock

united by a powerful sense of solidarity, marched on Newport, Monmouthshire. Troops killed around twenty of them, bloodshed that inspired many working people to be resolutely militant in their dealings with employers. The Chartist movement itself divided into differing streams in the 1840s and 1850s which evolved into the new opposition politics.

Unrest in the countryside from 1815 to 1850 was aggravated by poor harvests, famine, bank failures and unemployment. The poor law welfare rules were harshly enforced and in one notorious and emblematic case bailiffs seized the bed on which a sick man lay. Workhouses were built after 1832 to accommodate the poorest people but reports of cruelty behind the walls incited rioters to destroy two of the institutions, at Carmarthen and Narberth. Meanwhile, high rents and the large tithes demanded by the church rankled with farmers; and everyone hated the arrogant landlords who also sat in judgment on the magistrates' benches.

In short, rural Wales was already seething when the meagre harvests of 1838 and 1839 added despair to anger and ignited the Rebecca Riots. In 1839 crowds smashed the symbols of their oppression, the toll gates controlling the turnpike roads on which they moved their livestock and goods. Three years later they turned out again, stronger and angrier.

41. Down with the gates: Rebecca rioters attacked symbols of oppression including workhouses and weirs as well as toll gates. The Welsh Rioters. Engraving c.1843

Out *of* *the* blue

To ambitious churchmen Wales was for many years a threadbare province best avoided. In the eighteenth and early nineteenth centuries few of the bishops appointed to Wales had any connection with the country or spoke Welsh. Richard Watson, the bishop of Llandaff, lived in Cumbria and visited his see once a year. Many clergymen found comfort and dinner as chaplains to the landed families. Curates tended to be a ragged lot, poor or drunk or ill-educated. Thomas Burgess, bishop of Saint David's for more than twenty years from 1803, stood out as an exception in this tribe of indifferent clergy. He was an Englishman deeply interested in Welsh literature. Accordingly, he gave a tenth of his income to found a college at Lampeter to educate clergy.

The advance of nonconformity during the 1830s and 1840s coincided with a rapid and often chaotic eruption of industry. The church could not muster enough Welsh clergy to serve the numbers of people migrating from the country to the ironworks and collieries of south Wales. Chapels filled the gaps. Merthyr in 1840 had one church and a dozen chapels. The religious census of 1851 counted 1,180 churches in Wales and 2,769 chapels. It also revealed that half the people attended neither. In their chapels farmers, craftsmen, miners and labourers found equality, education and discussion that sharpened their political views. Nonconformity fostered resentment of landlord power and the tithes exacted by the church.

In the 1840s the government's concern over schooling in Wales, especially the question of teaching English, led to an inquiry that caused furious and enduring argument. There was a belief in official circles that the people were difficult, rebellious and riotous – hoisters of the red flag and wreckers of toll gates – because their lack of English alienated them from the church and reduced their respect for the law. An MP told the government that sending schoolmasters among the ill-educated and dangerous people of the valleys would be a cheaper remedy than despatching troops.

Three commissioners headed the inquiry. They were young and serious Anglican lawyers perfectly ignorant of Wales and its schools and people. Most of their 300 witnesses were Anglican clergy, some of whom were plainly resentful of the popularity of the chapels.

The inquiry report, published in three blue volumes in 1847, said that Welsh children were badly taught in deplorable buildings. There was much truth in this. But the report was an English judgment on Wales itself and played to the gallery of contemporary prejudice. The commissioners thought an ignorance of English was ignorance of everything. To their minds Wales was enslaved by a language that barred the way to moral progress.

Certainly, they found clean, sober and industrious people, but also grimy, drunken, backward creatures and promiscuous women: 'Want of chastity,' it was reported, 'is the giant sin of Wales.' An Anglican witness assured the inquiry that chapels were dens of sexual immorality. Thus, hidden between the prim blue covers, was the notorious sex bomb. To complete their picture the commissioners noted that parts of the landscape were bleak; and one tutted peevishly that he needed an umbrella: Wales was not only immoral but wet.

The report was indeed explosive. Its effects and meanings are still debated. Many reacted angrily and strongly rebutted it. In 1854 R.J. Derfel satirized the inquiry in his play Brad y Llyfrau Gleision, The Treachery of the Blue Books. The title alluded to 'the treachery of the long knives', a legendary feast at which the Saxon hosts stabbed their British guests.

As a libel the report inflamed relationships between the nonconformist majority and the Anglican minority. English commentators used the sexual slur to scourge Welsh people for 'the most savage barbarism' and 'animal habits.' The Times in 1860 called the Welsh language 'the curse of Wales.' Reactions in Wales underlined sensitivity to English sneering and to the stigma awarded to Welsh.

The report's conclusion, that salvation for the Welsh lay through English, was naturally accepted in England where the highly literate nature of Wales was not understood. It was also accepted by many in Wales hurt and shamed by the commissioners' views. These included some nonconformist leaders who believed Wales should earn respectability as an exemplary English-speaking sabbatarian society. There was a strong opinion that Wales needed an educated middle class and its own university to achieve equality with England.

On the other hand resentment of the Blue Books also intensified feelings of patriotism. Perhaps the report coloured the thoughts of Evan James of Pontypridd who in 1856 set out his love for his country in his song Hen Wlad fy Nhadau. In its attack the report bundled together the Welsh language, patriots, Methodists and all dissenters. Hitherto politically inert, Methodists in the 1860s began to join their fellow nonconformists in action for electoral reform.

Nonconformity emerged as the matrix of Welshness and culture. The old myths were discarded and a new story of radical and nonconformist Wales was written into the national script. Through its growing authority and the thrilling performances of celebrated preachers, nonconformity established its own palimpsest of the country's image. Victorian Wales emerged as a chapel-garrisoned country where temperance was strong and the sombre Welsh Sunday was a pillar. Huge chapel choirs made it famous everywhere as the 'land of

42. Blue Books satire: Sir James Kay-Shuttleworth, who headed the inquiry into education in Wales, was derided as Scuttleworth (also Gathercoal) with a coal scuttle on his head in Hugh Hughes's cartoons. His boots are off, revealing satanic cloven hooves. The three inquiry inspectors, Lingen, Johnson and Symons, have donkeys' ears. 1848

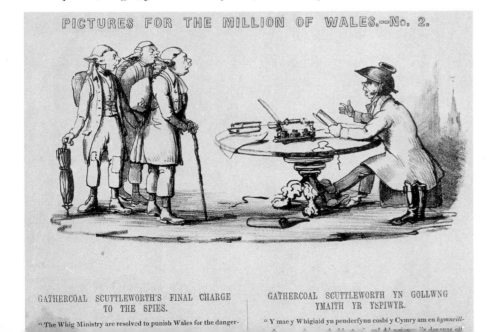

PICTURES FOR THE MILLION OF WALES.—No. 2.

GATHERCOAL SCUTTLEWORTH'S FINAL CHARGE TO THE SPIES.

"The Whig Ministry are resolved to punish Wales for the danger-

GATHERCOAL SCUTTLEWORTH YN GOLLWNG YMAITH YR YSPIWYR.

"Y mae y Whigiaid yn penderfynu cosbi y Cymry am en *hymneill*-

43. Concentration: The Deacons. John Petts, 1950

44. Memorial Chapel to William Ambrose 'Emrys', Porthmadog, c.1875

45. The Irish express: Thomas Telford's wrought-iron Menai road bridge, ancestor of all suspension bridges, opened to stage coaches in 1826. In the foreground is Stephenson's railway bridge, 1850. After Hugh Jones

song.' The chapels were profoundly creative influences, leaders of education, democracy and community life. They were also intransigent, narrow, sectarian and as disputatious as starlings.

Wales grew more prosperous with industrial expansion. The advancing railways required huge supplies of Welsh iron rails. Ebbw Vale had forged the rails of the pioneering Stockton–Darlington line in 1825. Isambard Brunel's brilliantly engineered line from Merthyr to Cardiff inaugurated the railway age in Wales in 1841. Robert Stephenson's tubular bridge over the Menai Strait opened in 1850 enabling trains to run directly from London to the Dublin steamers at Holyhead. Many roads, railways and bridges in Wales served London's strategic need to reach Ireland efficiently.

In a daring entrepreneurial stroke in 1839 the marquess of Bute ploughed his fortune into docks that opened the way to Cardiff's tremendous growth as a world port. In the 1850s Welsh coal production outstripped that of iron. The Royal Navy's decision in 1851 to fuel warships with Welsh steam coal launched the mining era in south Wales. In the 1860s Lord Bute and the engineer David Davies of Llandinam reached rich and hitherto inaccessible seams deep beneath the pastoral Rhondda. New railways delivered coal to Cardiff, Swansea and Newport; and slate from the quarries of Blaenau Ffestiniog, Llanberis and Bethesda to Porthmadog and Caernarfon. Industrial Wales became a player in the imperial and financial world, a breeder of tycoons.

All this happened with amazing speed. The coalfield took on its iconic appearance. Colliery winding gear, brick chimneys and

46. Saltwater city: the Bute docks made Cardiff the energy focus of the Victorian world. Wilson, 1849

48.

49.

50. Young pioneer: Henry Davies, aged five, left, with his mother, sister and brother, sailed in the Mimosa with the first Welsh migrants to Patagonia. His mother and two siblings died during the voyage. Henry was adopted

railways occupied the steep and smoky valleys. Terraces rose in amphitheatrical tiers. Coal waste became black and brooding hills. Miners' halls, pubs and chapels commanded street and argument. Physical transformation mirrored the evolution of a remarkable and vigorous society. The country was shaped by great surges of migration, in and out.

In common with millions of other Europeans, tens of thousands of migrants sailed from Wales to north America. In 1890 more than 100,000 Welsh people lived in the United States. Others made the voyage to Australasia. In 1865 some sailed to found a new Wales in Patagonia. Many left for the cities of England.

Significantly, however, in the sixty years from 1851 around 360,000 people travelled from their farms and villages in the Welsh countryside to the coalfield where they found an alternative to America, a livelihood and a culture in their own country. This rural influx put its decidedly Welsh and Welsh-speaking stamp on the coal valleys. Welsh literature, poetry and journalism flourished; but Welsh, though widely spoken, was not taught in schools.

At the same time, opportunities for work in the pits attracted numerous migrants from Ireland and England, especially from Somerset, Wiltshire and Gloucester. The Rhondda valleys became the most intensively-mined district on earth. Pontypridd, at the valleys' base, grew quickly into a strongly English-accented town.

The sheer scale of English immigration and Welsh emigration eroded the predominance of Welsh. In the early 1850s two-thirds of the people spoke Welsh, for most of them their only language. The numbers of Welsh-speakers actually increased, from 750,000 in 1851 to 930,000 in 1901. In 1911 there were a record 977,000, but for the first time they were a minority, under forty-four per cent, a decline that continued through the twentieth century.

Poverty, shortage of land and oppressive

50814. Aberystwyth College. FF & Co.

51. College
by the sea

52. Educating Wales: staff
at the university college in
Aberystwyth, c.1890

landlords multiplied grievances in rural Wales. In the elections in 1859 some Anglican gentry insisted that their tenant farmers vote for them; and a Cardiganshire landowner told her chapel-faithful tenants to attend church or quit their farms. The electoral reforms of 1867, however, ensured that small farmers and industrial workers had a resonant voice in towns like Merthyr, Cardiff and Swansea. In the watershed election of 1868 Merthyr voted Henry Richard into the Commons, the first powerful Welsh nonconformist in parliament.

In the same election Thomas Gee, the peppery Denbigh publisher, directed his venom at the owners of large estates. The election gave the Liberals twenty-one of the thirty-three Welsh parliamentary seats, beginning the era of Liberal majority in Wales that lasted until 1922. Some landlords retaliated by evicting their tenant farmers.

Protest flared in the countryside in the

1880s. Farmers refused to pay tithes to the church and the authorities sent troops to back the police in controlling demonstrators. The Vale of Clwyd was the heart of the 'tithe wars.' The people were embittered, too, by the bullying of gamekeepers and land agents. Meanwhile landowners stuffed tenancy agreements with illegal clauses and, as magistrates, administered the game laws with severity.

Change came with the legislation of 1888 which removed much of the landowners' power and transferred it to the new elected county councils. The storms on the land abated but nonconformists continued their struggle to disestablish the church in Wales, to separate it from the church of England.

From the valleys coal trains rumbled to the ports day and night. Cardiff swelled like a banqueting alderman. Its multi-racial dockland quarter, the Tiger Bay of fact and fiction, was also known to newspapermen as Hell's Acre.

53. *Green, green grass of home ground: Sardis Road, Pontypridd. The Rugby Match by Ronald H.J. Lawrence, 1984*

In a collision of titans David Davies of Llandinam, angered by Lord Bute's extortionate freight charges, built rival docks at Barry in the 1880s. In time these outstripped Cardiff in the quantity of coal shipped out. Every day scores of shouting and waving dealers in the Cardiff Coal Exchange fixed the price of coal; and here in 1907 the world's first million-pound deal was struck.

Caught up in the modernizing urge of the times Wales created its own, defiantly Welsh, versions of British structures. From the 1840s to the 1860s a national movement raised money for a Welsh university college which opened as 'the college by the sea' at Aberystwyth in 1872. Twenty-one years later the federal University of Wales was founded, with colleges at Cardiff and Bangor as well as Aberystwyth. In the 1870s pressure grew for the building of a national library and museum. The resurgent Welsh nationalism of this period was essentially cultural, not political, and expressed itself in a strong stream of literature, journalism, publishing and in the development of schools. As a musical accompaniment Hen Wlad fy Nhadau was fashioned into the popular national anthem.

Counterpart institutions were founded to promote sport. The Football Association of Wales was founded in 1876 and the Welsh Rugby Union five years later. The English public school game of rugby entered Wales through the middle classes and was enthusiastically adopted by the mining villages. Stiff nonconformists condemned it as the devil's mischief. In the Swansea valley chapel members sawed down the goalposts before a game. But rugby flourished as an expression of Welshness. The seductive notion that Wales had a 'Celtic genius' for rugby football was soon embroidered into the national legend.

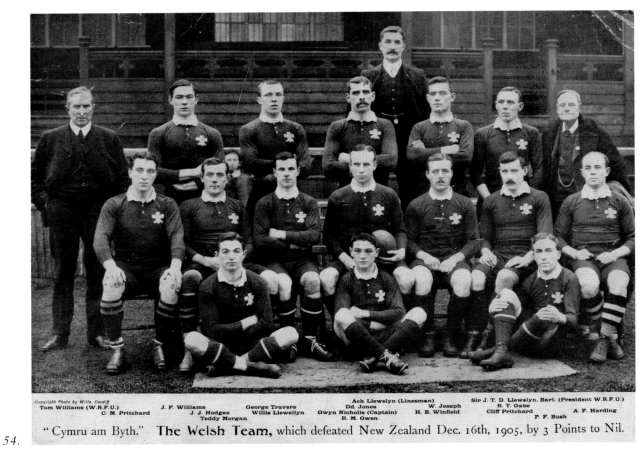

Copyright Photo by Wills, Cardiff

Tom Williams (W.R.F.U.)   J. F. Williams   George Travers   Ack Llewelyn (Linesman)   W. Joseph   Sir J. T. D. Llewelyn, Bart. (President W.R.F.U.)
C. M. Pritchard   J. J. Hodges   Willie Llewellyn   Dd. Jones   R. T. Gabe
Teddy Morgan   Gwyn Nicholls (Captain)   H. B. Winfield   Cliff Pritchard   A. F. Harding
R. M. Owen   P. F. Bush

"Cymru am Byth." **The Welsh Team,** which defeated New Zealand Dec. 16th, 1905, by 3 Points to Nil.

54.

Angry summers & bitter winters

The great strike of the Penrhyn quarry workers in north Wales between 1900 and 1903 was the longest industrial dispute in British history, a showdown between castle and cottage. Lord Penrhyn, the boss, was autocratic, Anglican and Tory. The workers were radical, nonconformist and Welsh-speaking. Lord Penrhyn held them in contempt and eventually humiliated them. Such bitter industrial struggle became a characteristic of most of the twentieth century in Wales.

In the Edwardian years, however, coal, metalworking and shipping created unprecedented prosperity in Cardiff, Swansea, Newport, Pontypridd, Llanelli, Neath, Wrexham and other towns. Cardiff swaggered as 'the Welsh metropolis' and built so grandly in Portland stone on its spacious riverside meadows that people talked of 'the Welsh Washington.'

Rugby football, meanwhile, played an heroic accompaniment to this swell of wealth and power. Between 1900 and 1911 the national team wore golden boots and won the Triple Crown six times. In a legendary encounter at

Cardiff Arms Park in 1905 Wales beat New Zealand and the embers glowed for a century.

The extraordinary religious fervour that raged in Wales in 1904-5 filled chapel pews and temperance ranks. Wales at that time counted 4,280 chapels. Sunday schools registered record numbers. Most of those recruited in the 'great revival' leaked away after a few years but in the meantime nonconformist enthusiasm was a factor in the election of 1906. This was the famous landslide in which the Liberals captured every seat in Wales apart from Keir Hardie's Labour fortress in Merthyr.

As chancellor of the exchequer forty-three-year-old David Lloyd George embarked on his creative years at the top of British politics. His 'people's budget' of 1909 pioneered the welfare state, part of his political engineering that built a bridge between the late Victorian and Edwardian age and the modern era.

The many thousands of young men who poured into the booming coalfield grew increasingly impatient and militant in their dealings with the hard-nosed coal owners. The South Wales Miners Federation, founded in 1898, was 120,000-strong when it affiliated ten years later with the rising Labour Party. The owners' refusal to pay decent wages and improve mine safety precipitated conflict. Rioting flared in Tonypandy in 1910. Shops were attacked and a miner killed after a clash with police. Winston Churchill, the home secretary, ordered troops to the Rhondda, an action so unpopular in Wales that cinema audiences into the 1950s jeered Churchill's appearances on newsreels. A seamen's strike in Cardiff in 1911 was followed by a railway strike in Llanelli where soldiers shot dead two innocent men.

55. Law enforcement: police at the Rink during Tonypandy strike 1910

56. Street in Tonypandy after riot, 1910, shops boarded up

57. Mountain climber: young Lloyd George

58. Landmark of the twentieth century: Lloyd George introduced national insurance in 1911, highly popular in Wales

THE STAMP THAT WANTS A LOT OF LICKING

AND THE MAN

*59. Include me in: enthusiasm for the fight, 1914.
Queue outside recruiting office*

The valleys seemed to be a crucible of class warfare. Hardline miners imbibed radical politics at Ruskin, the working men's college in Oxford, and at the Central Labour College in London. One of them, the marxist Noah Ablett, wrote his revolutionary text The Miners' Next Step, calling for workers' control of the pits. All but one per cent of Welsh coal was hewn by hand and the dangers inherent in digging it were underlined by the disaster

60. The dragon roars as the Kaiser runs: Y Ddraig Goch a Ddyry Gychwyn. J. Kelt Edwards, 1916

at Senghennydd, the worst in Welsh mining history, in which 439 men died. In that year of 1913 record coal production paid outstanding dividends to shareholders.

In September 1914, six weeks after the outbreak of war, Lloyd George declared that the fighting was in defence of the 'little five-foot-five nations' of Europe reeling under the German onslaught. His words resonated in five-foot-five Wales. Men and women, chapels and churches, miners and poets – all identified cheerfully with the cause. The number of men who enlisted in Wales was greater, as a proportion of the population, than that in England and Scotland, some 280,000 in all. A Welsh division was raised in 1914 and Welsh units distinguished themselves in battles along the Western front. In 1917 an empty eisteddfod chair movingly symbolized the sacrifice of the young: the winning poet had been killed in action.

Some in Wales betrayed the civilized values they claimed the troops were fighting for. They hounded an elderly German professor from

61. The sweet post-prandial cigar: Lloyd George in Cricieth

THE RIGHT HON. D. LLOYD GEORGE M. P,
AT HOME

Copyright   M. Roberts Series

62. Country house shooting party,
Montgomeryshire, c.1885

Aberystwyth, drove out another who had a German wife and meted harsh punishment to conscientious objectors.

As munitions minister and then secretary for war Lloyd George urged greater ferocity and a fight to the finish. Wales followed his career with pride. He was fifty-three when he became prime minister in December 1916 and set up a Downing Street establishment strongly Welsh in character and often Welsh in speech. As 'the man who won the war' he called an election in December 1918 and his Liberal-Tory coalition government won easily.

The social landscape of Wales in the winter of 1918 differed profoundly from that of the summer of 1914. Forty thousand Welshmen had been killed. The changes wrought by industrialized total war made the Edwardian world seem very distant, a vanished age.

The old order in the countryside withered as the squires saw their political power steadily weakened by the widening of the vote and their purses emptied by the cost of running estates. The persistent enmity of chapels and nonconformist newspapers also soured the pleasures of land ownership. In a great

sell-off from 1918 to 1922 the Welsh gentry
disposed of a quarter of their land. Many
of their tenants burdened themselves with
heavy mortgages to buy farms at inflated
prices and consequently suffered severely
in the depression of the 1920s and 1930s.
Country mansions assumed new roles as
schools and nursing homes; or simply fell
into ruin. The fading gentry rested upon
their memories of four centuries of power
and deference.

In 1920 an increasingly secular Wales gave
an old quarrel a decent burial: the Anglican
church in Wales was disestablished. It ceased
to be the state religion and became one
denomination among others. Its bishops
sat no more in the House of Lords and after
eight centuries no longer swore obedience
to Canterbury.

The chapels in those post-war years
dwindled as young people shook off the
grip of hidebound deacons and found more
relevance in union meetings, political lectures
and libraries; and innocent fun in cinemas,
seaside Sundays, pubs and the rugby ground.
The venomous stories of Caradoc Evans
scorned the puritanism and pomposity
of chapel elders and made him the most
notorious Welsh writer of his time.

The cruellest of false dawns opened
the 1920s in Wales. At first the output of a
record number of 272,000 miners produced
astonishing profits. But depression struck like
an aggressive wasting disease. Wales paid
heavily for having so much economic cargo
in one ship. The coal empire collapsed. The
end-of-war settlement forced Germany to
deliver coal as reparation payment to France
and Italy which had been major buyers of
Welsh coal. The Royal Navy, the original

Decline and fall:
63. top, Bertholey, Llantrisaint, Mon, 1997
64. bottom, Tegfynydd, Llanfallteg, Carms, 1998

champion of Welsh steam coal, launched
its first oil-powered ships in 1912 and
world shipping followed suit. The fall in Welsh
coal exports was matched by the decline in
shipments of Welsh steel and tinplate as the
United States, Belgium, Australia and others
developed their own industries.

Slump, unemployment and militancy gnawed at the government's strength. The nonconformist embrace of the Liberal cause grew flaccid and Labour's support multiplied. Lloyd George's concentration on foreign affairs was no help to his party at home; and there was some distaste for his presidential manner and trafficking in honours. In October 1922, after seventeen continuous years in government, six of them as prime minister, he resigned. In the ensuing general election Labour won eighteen of the thirty-five Welsh seats, and 142 overall, becoming the chief opposition. Thereafter the Liberal party crumbled like a sandcastle lapped by the tide.

From the mid-1920s unemployment and exodus brought Wales to its knees. In fourteen years from 1925 the country's population shrank by a quarter of a million. Tens of thousands quit the shrivelling valleys for Dagenham, Coventry, Slough and Luton. Penniless men walked to London to seek work. The nine-day British general strike of 1926 had a brutal aftermath in Wales. The miners stayed out and their communities joined them in determined solidarity until, after seven months, hunger drove the men back to work.

In 1928 The Times reported from Merthyr: 'These out of work miners are cultivated people with self-respect and pride in home cleanliness and feel the degradation of their sudden poverty ... they are starving; not starving outright but gradually wasting away through lack of nourishment.' Later a study recommended that Merthyr should be abandoned as a hopeless case and its people rehoused on the coast.

65. *Defiance: striking miners at Cwmparc, Rhondda, 1936*

66. *The meagre years: miners off to work in the early morning at a mid-Rhondda colliery, 1936*

The valleys that once mined a third of the world's coal produced under three per cent of it in 1929. Cardiff's docks and shipping were shadows of what they had been. Only Swansea, serving the western anthracite pits, still bustled. In south Wales in 1932 150,000 men were out of work. In Rhondda and its sister valleys more than half the men had no job. Hardship gripped the farming communities, too.

Yet a strong thread of comradeship and self-reliance ran through those desperate years. Medical aid societies, co-operative shops, miners' institutes, home-made entertainment and cinemas helped to make hard times bearable. Many local councils improved both health and morale by clearing slums, providing sanitation, parks, school meals and milk. By drawing together, people endured and created their own legend. The anguish of these times was movingly expressed by Gwyn Thomas, Bert Coombes, Idris Davies and other novelists and poets who formed part of a distinctive stream of Welsh writing in English.

Through it all the Labour party and the unions grew as the people's voice. The radicalism that formerly energized the Liberal cause was directed increasingly to Labour. In the 1929 general election the Liberals won only nine Welsh seats and fifty-nine overall. Labour won more than two-fifths of the Welsh vote. One of the new MPs, elected for Ebbw Vale, was thirty-two-year-old Aneurin Bevan, who had worked in the pits at fourteen. The miners' leader James Griffiths, a collier for seventeen years and, like Bevan, a product of the Central Labour College, became MP for Llanelli in 1936.

67. Wales and socialism:
James Griffiths, c.1956

68. 'Something must be done':
King Edward VIII
in south Wales, 1936

69. The power of speech:
Aneurin Bevan campaigning
at Corwen Pavilion, 1951

'I could not vote Tory. It is wrong'

70. *Operation Pied Piper:*
boys evacuated to Oswestry,
1939

In 1939, as they had in 1914, Welsh people
volunteered wholeheartedly for the fighting
services and war work. Mass unemployment
ended and wages rose. This time, of course,
there was total war. Air raids killed hundreds
of people in Wales, seriously damaged Cardiff
and smashed the heart of Swansea. But even
in war's bleakest times men planned for the
future. Welsh Labour figures like Bevan and
Griffiths campaigned for a post-war Britain
reconstructed on socialist lines, with public
ownership and social security, a health service
and decent housing. In Wales especially the
memory of the depression hardened the
common resolve to defeat poverty and
restore dignity.

71. *Top:*
Labels and gas masks:
apprehensive boys arrive
in Newtown, 1939

72. *Bottom:*
Morning after:
Blitz damage,
Swansea, 1941

Loss & renewal

Labour's overwhelming victory in 1945 included the winning of twenty-five of the thirty-six Welsh seats. James Callaghan and George Thomas became Cardiff MPs. As ministers in Clement Attlee's government, James Griffiths, minister of national insurance, and Aneurin Bevan, minister of health, established the welfare state on ground laid out forty years earlier by Lloyd George. More than any other achievement, the national health service they created stood as Labour's enduring monument.

The government emphasized centralized economic and social planning. Miners celebrated the fulfilment of their fifty-year dream as coal came into public ownership in 1947. Steel was nationalized in 1951, a time of swelling optimism. A decade later steel manufacture boomed at Shotton and Llanwern. In the 1960s the steelworks at Port Talbot paid such handsome wages that it was called 'treasure island.' From 1960 Milford Haven developed as a major European oil refining centre, a terminus for increasingly gigantic tankers.

The first Severn bridge opened in 1966, a handsome work of art in the landscape and the new gateway to Wales. The government moved the Royal Mint from London to Llantrisant and the Driver and Vehicle Licensing Centre to Swansea. There were more jobs for white-collar staff and also for women who, after the war, became two-fifths of the labour force. Newtown in mid-Wales was actively developed as a hub of business and housing to stem depopulation in the countryside.

The other side of this progress was a chronicle of unremitting reverses. People still quit rural Wales for want of a living. Quarrying in the north became vestigial. Cardiff Coal Exchange closed in 1958, and for the lack of markets the city's coal exports finished in 1964. Fifty thousand mining jobs dried up in the ten years to 1969. But hopes that mining could somehow survive as a premier industry flickered tantalizingly. In 1966, cruelly emphasising the terrible price in suffering that mining so often exacted, a monstrous heap of coal waste on the slopes above Aberfan collapsed and engulfed the village school.

Until the 1960s little of the political debate turned on specifically Welsh concerns. Many believed with Aneurin Bevan that after the horrors of the depression what mattered most was a dignified living for Welsh people in an integrated and centrally-directed socialist Britain. Many shared his hostility to any whisper of a Welsh parliament.

In 1957 the Conservative government overrode the objections of every Welsh MP

73. The price of water: Capel Celyn villagers take their case to Liverpool, 1956

and supported the damming of the Tryweryn valley in Merionethshire and the drowning of Capel Celyn village. The reservoir was to provide Liverpool with water for its industrial expansion and profit. The government's contempt for Welsh opinion shocked many; and Tryweryn played its part in the nationalist awakening in the 1960s.

Reactions to the 1961 census made a political issue of the Welsh language.

74. Before the flood: selling cattle in the last sale at Gwerngaeau farm in the Tryweryn valley, 1957

The figures revealed that 656,000 people, twenty-six per cent of the population, spoke Welsh, and that the language was declining rapidly. It enjoyed scant public status and only a tenuous place in law. In 1962 the poet and dramatist Saunders Lewis, a founder of Plaid Cymru in 1925, called for revolutionary action to secure Welsh in the life of Wales. In a radio lecture, Tynged yr Iaith, the Fate of the Language, he warned that without such action the language would die. His stark analysis led to the founding of the Welsh Language Society and a militant campaign to bring Welsh into official use.

Campaigners made the point that Welsh was conspicuously absent from official display and that Welsh-speakers lacked the means to deal with government and administration in their native language. It was a question of justice. They asked the authorities to provide bilingual forms and vehicle and television licences. They also called for bilingual road signs. The courts fined and jailed protesters who refused to buy licences and damaged English-only road signs. Twenty-one magistrates caused consternation when their consciences led them to pay the fine of the leading campaigner, Dafydd Iwan.

76. Catalyst: Saunders Lewis, 1973

Although the Welsh Language Act of 1967 gave Welsh 'equal validity' with English it was widely considered inadequate and

75. Saying what language means: a march in support of bilingual road signs, Aberystwyth, 1971

led to further action. Many saw the language struggle as a civil rights movement or a Welsh version of the idealistic protest sweeping Europe and America. Ultimately it was the most effective civil disobedience campaign in Britain in the second half of the twentieth century, and some have drawn a parallel with the struggle for votes for women.

James Griffiths, meanwhile, had persuaded Labour to take the devolutionary plunge and, when the party came to power in 1964, Harold Wilson appointed him the first secretary of state for Wales. At Griffiths's insistence Wilson also created a Welsh Office, an expanded version of the Welsh Affairs branch of the Home Office set up by Winston Churchill in 1951. Under Griffiths and his successors

the Welsh Office inevitably accrued responsibilities and made Cardiff the political focus in Wales.

In the Carmarthen by-election of 1966 Gwynfor Evans won Plaid Cymru's first parliamentary seat. The party's credibility was further enhanced in the 1974 general election when Dafydd Elis-Thomas and Dafydd Wigley became MPs. Over the next thirty or more years they contributed significantly to Welsh politics. Meanwhile, in 1969, the Labour government had responded to the nationalist breeze by staging the investiture of the Prince of Wales in an effort to please Welsh sentiment; and also by setting up a royal commission, the traditional time-consumer, to consider devolution.

Processions and protests calling for wider public use of Welsh peaked in the late 1960s and early 1970s; and 'Remember Tryweryn' was a popular slogan. Meanwhile, the ever stubborn Gwynfor Evans made his political breakthrough in Carmarthen, 1966

77. Cardiff 1970

78. Aberystwyth 1971

79.

80.

The 1971 census, showing that Welsh-speakers formed just under twenty-one per cent of the population, sharpened the sense of cultural crisis. The language campaign intensified and protesters set their sights on winning a Welsh television channel. During these years new bilingual schools were opened to meet an expanding parental demand for education through Welsh. The language question was an essential element in debate about the nature of Wales and part of the process that created modern Welsh politics.

In 1964 the BBC in Wales was awarded its own television wavelength and began broadcasting programmes in English and Welsh within the British network hours. Welsh was no longer banished to the far reaches of the night. The question of sharing the wavelength, complicated by the transmission problems in a mountainous land, led to years of controversy, some of it bitter. As a national cultural organization committed to serving two language communities in one country BBC Wales was inevitably caught up in thorny political arguments.

It was also reporting the struggles of miners and steel workers engaged in their acrimonious twenty-year war to defend industries that were the core of a long-established way

81. Solidarity: the strong support that women gave their men was a characteristic of the bitter miners' strike of 1984–85

of life. Miners won their strike in 1972 and two years later brought down Edward Heath's Conservative government. But pits and steelworks remained overmanned and uncompetitive. They continued to close and jobs drained away. In 1975 Michael Foot, MP and successor to Bevan, told people in his Ebbw Vale constituency that steel-making in their valley was over, that they had reached the end of a particular history. In an angry scene they roared that he had betrayed them; but he told a truth that most politicians and steel bosses shrank from.

The question of an assembly for Wales was put by the Labour government in a referendum in 1979. The proposal was decisively rejected. Labour itself was split between those who saw in devolution a better way of managing Welsh affairs and those who spied a Trojan horse with a belly full of nationalists.

Later that year, seeing disarray in Wales, Margaret Thatcher's new Tory government reneged on its pledge to launch the Welsh television channel S4C. It quickly re-honoured it when Gwynfor Evans threatened to starve himself to death in its cause.

The 1970s and the 1980s were a time of torment and industrial strife as a new economic order supplanted the old.

82. The last payday at Gelli Ceidrim Colliery, 1957

The government ruthlessly cut jobs in the coal and steel industries to put an end to the chaotic uncertainty caused by management and unions. As part of the new order the government set its face against overmanning in steel and in the four years to 1983 cut jobs in the industry by seventy per cent. Steel manufacture in Wales is today significant and efficient.

At the time of the cuts there were fears that unemployment might ignite social disorder. Arthur Scargill, the NUM leader, thought in 1984 that the miners could topple Mrs Thatcher's government, as they had beaten Heath's ten years earlier. He was living in the past. This time the strike was declared illegal, lasted eleven months and ended in defeat for the miners and ruin for their union.

From 1985 there were pit closures on a large scale and mining in Wales entered its final chapter. In valleys and villages with legendary names the colliery hooter fell silent. The last pit in the Rhondda, at proudly-militant Maerdy, closed in 1990 and the people held a wake. In an echo of Noah Ablett's dream, miners bought Tower colliery in the Cynon valley in 1995 and ran it themselves, flying a defiant red flag from the pithead gear, a last stand. But the wealth had been wrung from the seams and the purpose of a people had suddenly ended. It was hard to believe that Welsh miners were almost extinct. A few became guides in pit museums.

One morning, in a primary school in the Rhondda, a former miner started talking to a class of boys and girls. He wore his helmet and lamp and pit boots. He was there to tell them of a Welsh genesis, their parents' and grandparents' story, and their own history. Where to begin? He held in his palm a gleaming black fragment. 'This,' he said to the wide-eyed children, 'is coal.'

83. Four Colliers, Valerie Ganz, c.1980

*84. The Senedd
Debating Chamber,
Cardiff Bay, 2006*

A point *of* departure

In 1979 Wales had voted four to one against a devolved assembly. Eighteen years later it narrowly voted in favour, the dramatic modern turning point in the Welsh story, and, as ever in Wales, a cliffhanger.

Many who favoured an assembly in 1979 were devastated by the outcome, but some said there would be business as usual; and they were right: the question did not go away. Rather, a more thoughtful examination of the arguments helped to strengthen Welsh politics. In 1979 devolution had been proposed by a tired and retreating Labour government as Labour voices bellowed opposition to it. In 1997 the assembly had the imprimatur of the popular New Labour government and considerable support from the young. By that time, too, Britain had been in Europe for almost two decades, an experience that in Wales changed the political context in which devolution was considered.

Much happened in the interval between the two votes. Plaid Cymru ceased to frighten the horses and became a respectable middle-class player in the political discourse. The sense of crisis that fired language campaigns in the 1960s and 1970s moderated as the issue was addressed. S4C began in 1982. Bilingual forms and signs became part of the paperwork as Welsh developed its public face. Commerce found value in using more Welsh. There was a sense of live and let live, a growing ease with a diversity of which Welsh was a part.

The appetite for Welsh-language education grew and, significantly, many parents who had no Welsh wanted their children to know the language. The first Welsh-medium secondary school opened in 1956. Today there are fifty-four such schools where more than half the foundation subjects are taught through Welsh. There are 455 Welsh-speaking primary schools, twenty-nine per cent of the total. The number of Welsh-speaking children began to increase.

During the tumultuous years from No to Yes, and into the twenty-first century, much that had been intrinsic and defining in Wales faded in the retreat from mining and steel. In the late 1940s manual workers formed threequarters of the British population and expressed their political power through unions which embodied activist traditions and produced a stream of political figures. Today less than two-fifths of British people are manual workers; and with the decline of unions and the growth of the service and knowledge economy the political source that nurtured the tradition of one dominant party in Wales has dwindled.

In this and in many other ways the landscape was transformed. When we consider the century that has passed since the National Library was founded in 1907 we see a world turned upside down, and also a determination to make a new one. In the 1970s coal waste was hauled down from Aberfan to Cardiff to fill old docks and make foundations for the aspirational structures of the future. The Welsh Assembly that began work in 1999 was the first such conclave since Owain Glyn Dŵr's parliament six centuries earlier. Amid discordance and ambivalence about its powers it began to make its way.

In 2006 the assembly's new workshop, the Senedd, opened in Cardiff Bay, a graceful and translucent pavilion facing the Severn Sea, the forum and junction for all the intersecting worlds of Wales. In 2007 it acquired legislative sinew, the first opportunity in centuries for the people of Wales to create a corpus of Welsh law. A dozen years earlier such an exciting reality and heavy responsibility had been barely imaginable. There was throughout Wales a sense that, for many reasons, one long journey had ended and another was just beginning.

Next page:

85. Rocks and hard places: Pen yr Ole Wen, Capel Curig, c.1999

86. Wales revealed: Humphrey Llwyd drew the first printed map of Wales, Cambriae Typus. It was published in 1573, five years after his death

Ynys Adar .1. insula auium
olim; nunc verò, ynys Moyl
Rhoniaid, 1. insula
phocarum, B.
Yſleryd. D.
Adros. L.

CAMBRI AE TYPVS
Auctore
HVMFRE
DO LHV:
YDO
Denbigienſe Cam:
brobritāno.

Mona inſula. L.
Angleſey. A.
Mon. B.

Lymnus Ptol.
ynys Enlhi. B.
Bardaſey. A.

...M SIVE HIBERNICVM MARE

...IDH, Britannis,

...HE OCEANE, Anglis.

Witness

The National Library of Wales harvests the raw material of experience and expression that shape the country's history. Manuscripts, books, paintings, photographs, maps, music, recordings, newspapers and films, amounting to millions of volumes and items, bear witness to countless human stories. They form an immense granary of thought and record for two cultures, endlessly replenished, a vital link between the long-ago and the future.

The library is unique in the sweep of its gathering, with its view over Welsh and English literature and publishing, its political archives, medieval parchments, church and manorial records, the work, letters and diaries of scholars, poets, sportsmen, statesmen, soldiers, actors and travellers. It is also an audio-visual centre, a remarkable photographic archive and, significantly and actively, a magnificent national picture gallery.

It is, above all, a place of discovery and surprise where the past is not distant but accessible; where, as the following pages show, the people tell their story in their own words and images.

LOVE AND SURVIVAL

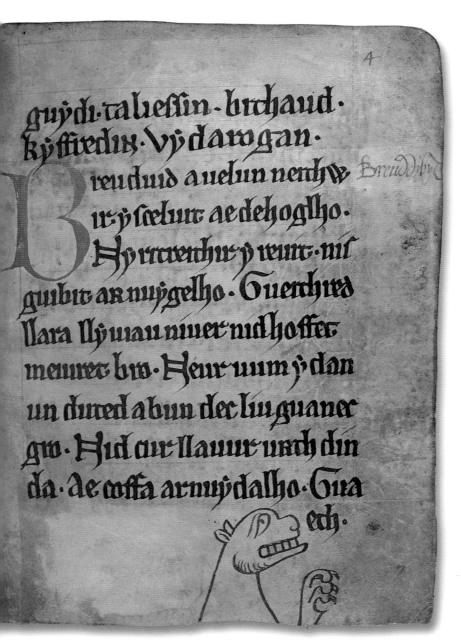

*87. Dandy doodle: when a text intruded
into the bottom margin of a page,
as here in the Black Book, medieval
scribes often added an amusing drawing
(actual size)*

The Black Book of Carmarthen is the senior book of Wales, the oldest gathering of Welsh poetry and a remarkable survivor. Most medieval books were lost to rot and rodents, fire and war – and the grim destroyers of the Reformation. The Black Book, however, reached its refuge in the nation's library after a long and romantic journey, passed along the centuries like a sacred baton.

Only six-and-a-half inches high, a pocket-book with 108 parchment pages, it was compiled by a single scribe at Carmarthen priory, around 1250. Its beauty goes beyond its antiquity, for it is quite different from the usual run of manuscripts compiled by monks in religious houses. It is a personal anthology of favourite pieces, of poems sung by bards around the fire, stories of kings, battles and heroes, all harvested over the years by one man, for his own enjoyment, to read whenever he wanted. Some of the verses date from the ninth century, introducing us to King Arthur, Merlin and the fantastic world of the Mabinogion. It is a touchingly human document, a work of love, drawing

88.

us into the mind of a man in medieval Wales.

His pen-work remains bright. He started with a visually-stunning splash, his lettering majestic, with red and green capitals, but the writing shrank as he crammed more words onto the pages. Parchment was expensive and he had to make it last.

The book may have been at Carmarthen priory for three centuries until Henry VIII ordered the seizure of monastic wealth. In the 1530s the lawyer and scholar Sir John Price of Brecon was sent as an inspector to search monasteries. It seems he discovered the Black Book in the keeping of the treasurer of Saint David's cathedral. In the following century it passed into the hands of the visionary collector Robert Vaughan. In 1859 Vaughan's descendant willed the collection to William Watkin Edward Wynne, of Peniarth, near Tywyn, Merioneth, who in 1904 sold it to Sir John Williams. The collection became the foundation of the National Library and the Black Book is catalogued simply as Peniarth 1.

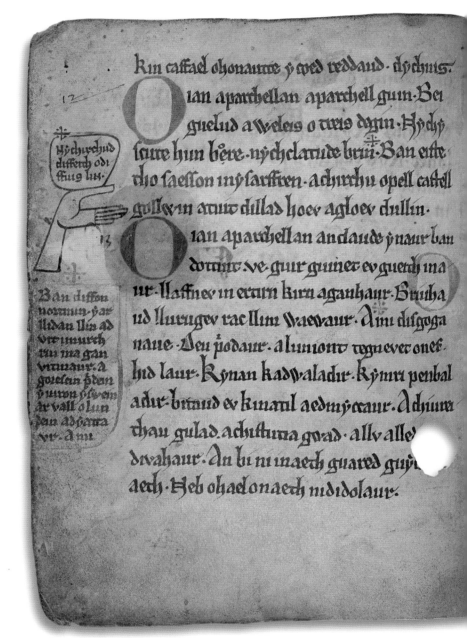

89. Showing his hand: the scribe has fun with another doodle

THE TOMBLESS KING

If King Arthur existed at all he may have been a British chief of the fifth or sixth century who fought Anglo-Saxon tribes penetrating Britain as the Roman tide receded. By the ninth century he was already a hero of Welsh legends, a repository of hope, the deathless warrior who would rise from slumber in a cave and restore the Welsh, the original Britons, to their sovereignty over all of Britain.

The tradition of a deliverer was an invigorating myth and a powerful theme in medieval poetry. Bards hailed Owain Glyn Dŵr as a returning Arthur. Henry Tudor's winning of the English crown at the battle of Bosworth seemed a plausible fulfilment of Welsh hopes. Thereafter the prophetic theme withered.

By that time writers in England had already shaped the attractive figure of Arthur into an English hero. A Norman poet had furnished him with a Round Table for knightly feasts. In the twelfth century

90. Birth of a legend: King Arthur in a medieval manuscript

Richard I identified himself with Arthur.
Europeans borrowed the legend for their
own literature. Sir Thomas Malory's brilliant
romance, Morte d'Arthur, written around 1470,
ensured an heroic future for the redeemer-king.

91. Lament for the leader: in Cara Wallia
derelicta, one of his painted inscriptions,
David Jones echoed Welsh grief at the
death of Llywelyn in 1282, the pain as
the prince's head was borne away on an
iron pike. David Jones's style of lettering
has an enduring influence on calligraphers

BLOOD AND THUNDER

Brut y Tywysogyon, the Chronicle of the
Princes, is a rich and remarkable source of
information about life in Wales in the six
centuries to the death of Llywelyn ap
Gruffudd in 1282. The account of the
200 years after 950 is a graphic horror story
of the murder and mutilation of chieftains.
The chronicle also indicates the spreading
use in Wales of the term Cymro: Welshman.
The original Latin chronicles kept by monks
were lost but three Welsh translations
survive, probably copied in the fourteenth
century in the busy scriptorium at Strata
Florida in Ceredigion. Like several other
Cistercian houses founded by the Normans,
this abbey was patronised by Welsh princes
and eventually came under Welsh control.

WHITE BOOK
AND RED

Whoever set down the eleven stories we call The Mabinogion was a literary star of the Middle Ages. These tales of Arthur and Merlin, monsters, princes, gods and maidens form a treasure of European literature. Known before the tenth century they were retold through the generations until an unknown writer scooped them up and saved them. They were collected around 1350 in The White Book of Rhydderch, which is in the National Library, and later in The Red Book of Hergest, now kept at Oxford. These stories from the long-ago might so easily have been lost. They survived the storms on flimsy rafts of parchment.

92. Magic Mabinogion: The Enchantment of Dyfed. Margaret Jones, c.1984

The Bala poet John Jones, Tegid, made a transcript of the Red Book and gave it to Charlotte, the young wife of the Dowlais ironmaster Sir John Guest. From 1838 she rendered the stories into English and published three handsome illustrated volumes in 1846, the first English translation. For a title she concocted the word Mabinogion, meaning tales, and as a convenient handle it endures.

It is a remarkable story. Charlotte married Sir John in 1835 when she was twenty-one. She studied Welsh, cutting against the grain of a gentry largely indifferent or hostile to the language. She already had a passion for Romantic literature. She was not fluent in Welsh and was helped in the translation by John Jones and the clergymen Thomas Price and Evan Jenkins. Her energy and organizing ability drove the exhausting project to fruition. The Mabinogion competed for her time with her frequent pregnancies: she had ten children. After her husband's death in 1852 she ran his ironworks. She died in 1895, aged eighty-three.

The tales of The Mabinogion are Pwyll Prince of Dyfed; Branwen daughter of Llŷr; Manawydan son of Llŷr; Math son of Mathonwy; The Dream of Macsen Wledig; Lludd and Llefelys; The Dream of Rhonabwy; Culhwch and Olwen; The Lady of the Fountain; Peredur son of Efrawg; Geraint son of Erbin. In 1948, a century after Charlotte Guest's translation, Gwyn Jones and Thomas Jones published an authoritative version drawn from the White Book.

93. The White Book of Rhydderch: Pwyll Prince of Dyfed

Pwyll pendeuic dyuet
a oed yn arglwyd ar seith
cantref dyuet. a threig
ylgweith yd oed yn arberth
prif lys idaw a dyuot yny
uryt ac yny uedwl mynet
y hela. Sef kyueir oe gywoeth
a uynnei y hela glynn cuch.
ac ef agychwynnwys y nos
honno o arberth ac acoeth llyst
ym penn llwyn diarwya. ac
yno y bu y nos honno. a thr
annoeth yn ieuengtit y dyd
kyuodi aoruc a dyuot y lynn
cuch i ellwng cwn dau ywet.
a chann y gorn adechreu dy
gyuor yr hela. a cherdet yn
ol y cwn ac ymgolli ay gydy
mdeithon. ac ual y byd yn
ymwarandaw allef yr erchw
ys. ef aglywei llef erchwys
arall. ac nit oedynt unllef.
a hynny yn dyuot yn erbyn
y erchwys ef. ac ef awelei la
nnerch ymywet onaew gu
astat. ac ual yd oed y erchwys
ef yn ymgael ac ystlys yllan
nerch ef awelei carw onaen
yr erchwys arall. a pharth a
pherued y llannerch llyma
yr erchwys aoed yny ol yn
ymordiwes ac ef. ac yny uw
yr llawr. ac yna edrych ohon
aw ef ar liw yr erchwys heb
hanbwyllaw edrych ar y carw.
ac or awelsei ef ohelgwn ybyt.
ny welsei cwn un lliw ac wynt.
Sef lliw oed arnunt claerwynn

llathreit. ac en clusteu y
gochwen. Ac ual y llathreu
y wynnet y cun y llathreu ro
chet y clusteu. ac ar hynny
at y cwn y doeth ef ...wa
yr erchwys alad ystac y carw
eynnderth allithyaw y erchw
ys ehunan ar y carw. ac ual
y byd yn llithaw y cwn. ef a
welei uarchauc yn dyuot
yn ol yr erchwys y ar uarch
erchlas mawr. a cho...
am y mynbygyl. ag...
thy... llwyt teu andaw
yn biw hela. ac ar h...
y marchawc adoeth
a dywedut ual...
unben heb ef
wytti ac ny chy...
rt. Ie heb ef aca...
arnat canysyd...
hyei. Unben heb e...
hygdawc uy annyscd a...
eisseu am hynny. A...
heb ynteu beth annyge...
froti adaw heb ynteu dy
anbydot dy llun atu ansy
werbyst. Pa ans...berbyt u...
ben awelsei ti arnat ...
welei ansyterbyst uwy...
or heb ef no gynn...
ysa alad ystlei ...cyu
erth. allithian dy erchwys
dy lunianab. hynny y heb
ef ansyberbyt oed. a hy
nyt yndialbyt a...
adwb heb ef...
anglot ytt guerth

in curia . & de curia habebit abum
suū & cliencis sui abum . Grans facet
regi ota opa sua exceptis trib; . scal
dario . dolabro . & ferro lancee . i. pen
gwayw . de illis : habebit merede
sui labouis . fab curie deber hie pmo
potui in comuno . i. keynon . fab cu
rie deber hie . iiii . d . de quolibet pso
ne a se in umcht posito & cu ab ipit eu
libauit . Ipe deber hie merede de fili
arum pncipis fabror sibi sbdtror .

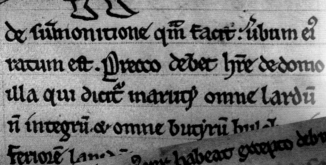

Recco uocat De jure pconis .
walensice kennat vaur engryt
ul comunis nuntius . i . & tocius prie
de sumonitione qm facit : ubum e
ratum est . Precco deber hie de domo
illa qui dicit marus omne lardū
ū integrū & omne butyrū hul-
feriore lan—
ciam el rex habeat goccepro debito in
morot . De ambro denidisi eat :

lib . ebed
bed . kym
im maal
3 libre sine
y tuno su
st libra .
i . dimid
—uits abstulerit?

The Laws of Hywel Dda formed a code
for living and helped to define Wales as a
country. Written originally in Welsh they
demonstrated that Wales could aspire to
its own national institutions. The rare
and charming thirteenth-century Latin
text shown here was perhaps a gift for
a senior official.

The pictures are delightful. The best-
drawn shows the king on his throne. Others
are rough depictions of dogs, cows, birds and
bees, creatures which had a legal value. A
queen bee, for example, was worth twenty-
four pence. There are also drawings of a
blacksmith, a falconer, a huntsman, a steward
with a dish and a couple kissing. One shows
a man tugging another's hair, an offence
punishable by a fine of a penny for each
hair pulled out by the root. Under the laws
a falconer was limited to three hornsful of
liquor with his meals: no more in case he
got drunk. Anyone selling a cat had to
guarantee that it was a good mouser
and did not caterwaul at the moon.

Far ahead of their time the Laws of Hywel
insisted on fair treatment for women and
acknowledged impotence and halitosis as
grounds for a marital separation. If a couple
parted the husband was awarded the family
pigs and his wife the sheep. The laws

94. Who goes there?
Sergeant with lance

95. The value
of a bird

covered boundary disputes and the duties of judges. They also set out the tasks of court bards, including the requirement to chant a stirring poem before a battle and the observance of strict etiquette when the bards recited privately to the queen: they had to sing quietly to avoid disturbing others.

96. A point of law: the king, with sceptre, in the Laws of Hywel Dda

97. Groom and saddle, and cook slaughtering a fowl

98. Kissing couple

THE GOLDEN CENTURY

No book written in Welsh before the mid-thirteenth century survives. But in the hundred years after 1250 monastery scribes copied a treasury of histories, laws, religious prose and poetry. More than fifty survive, including The Black Book of Carmarthen, The White Book of Rhydderch, the Hendregadredd Manuscript, the Book of Taliesin and the Book of Aneirin, which might be regarded as the 'big five' early books of Welsh poetry. The first four are in the National Library and the Aneirin is in Cardiff. The pioneer poets of Wales, Taliesin and Aneirin, were masters of taut and vivid imagery. Their verse rhythms were already a tradition when they were writing in the late sixth century.

99. The roots of poetry: the Book of Taliesin

SECRET OF THE WARDROBE

The Hendregadredd Manuscript was one of literature's missing links, lost for centuries and sensationally found in 1910. Its 126 pages, compiled from the late thirteenth century to the mid-fourteenth, probably at Strata Florida, contain the work of 'the poets of the princes', or gogynfeirdd, who praised the valour of Welsh leaders and spared no details of battlefield horror. Some of the writing is thought to be in the hand of Dafydd ap Gwilym. With The Red Book of Hergest the Hendregadredd Manuscript is a key source of twelfth-century court poetry. It was in Robert Vaughan's library but went missing and was found in a wardrobe in a disused bedroom at Hendregadredd, near Porthmadog, hence its name. Very few scholars knew anything about it. The Davies sisters of Gregynog bought it at auction in 1923 and gave it to the National Library.

100. The final part of Dafydd ap Gwilym's poem in praise of the rood screen at Carmarthen, in the Hendregadredd Manuscript

COLOUR WRITER

In his vivid masterpiece, History of the Kings of Britain, published around 1136, the storyteller Geoffrey of Monmouth presented the Welsh with a satisfyingly magnificent past. He described how ancient Britain was settled by Trojan migrants after the Greeks took Troy; and how King Arthur became a celebrated leader of British resistance to the Saxons. His imaginative tales of Arthur, Guinevere and Merlin enthralled his readers.

There is no evidence to support the claim in his preface that his source was an 'ancient book in the British tongue'; but possibly he drew on earlier chronicles written in Welsh. In any case his creative narrative was an influential and popular saga of a golden age, his characters delineated in strong and convincing colours. The stories blazed the path for history writers in the centuries ahead. They were later scorned but they were a good read.

Geoffrey wrote in Latin and around 200 copies of his manuscript survive in several countries. It had such appeal in Wales that it was translated into Welsh at least three times before the end of the thirteenth century.

There is a Welsh translation in the Black Book of Basingwerk, a fifteenth-century manuscript copied not at Basingwerk abbey in Flintshire but probably at Valle Crucis in Denbighshire. The binding is rare in that it retains its medieval wooden boards. It is also unusual in the scribes' use of blue-green ink.

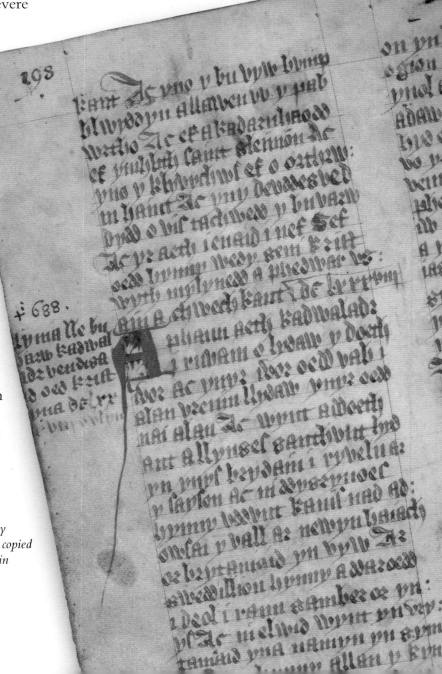

101. The glory that was Wales: tales spun by Geoffrey of Monmouth, copied c.1450 by Gutun Owain

102.
Black Book
of Basingwerk

A MEDIEVAL MIRROR

Gerald of Wales, known also as Giraldus Cambrensis, is one of the best guides to twelfth-century Wales. He had a journalist's eye for human detail, was sometimes misleading and invariably entertaining. He described a people with a firm sense of their country and ancestry, witty, musical and generous, devoted to their horses and weapons. They had pudding basin haircuts and polished their teeth with wool. Gerald thought they drank too much, made unreliable promises and were hobbled by political disunity.

Born in 1146 at Manorbier, the son of a Norman knight and a half-Welsh mother,

he felt too Norman for the Welsh, too Welsh for the Normans. Never self-effacing, he described himself as handsome and the best scholar in Wales. He was certainly a gifted Latin writer. He held the post of archdeacon of Brecon for twenty-eight years and tried in vain to be appointed archbishop of Saint David's. He travelled in Ireland and made four trips to Rome. His contacts with Welsh rulers made him useful to the English kings Henry II and Richard I.

In 1188 he and the archbishop of Canterbury toured Wales for seven weeks, recruiting men for the crusades, and along the way he gathered material for his fascinating

103. The traveller's eye: Gerald of Wales was a best-seller

104. Manorbier castle, Pembrokeshire, Gerald's birthplace, c.1840

Journey through Wales, written in 1191, and A Description of Wales, 1194. The latter is the single source of the inspiring prophecy uttered to Henry II by the old man of Pencader, that only the Welsh and their language would for ever answer for their corner of the earth. They are the last words of the book. Gerald died in 1223, aged seventy-seven. After the invention of printing his books were best-sellers.

A BUNDLE OF SOUND

105. Strata Florida: 'God bless the yew, for it is bliss/ To be the house where Dafydd is' – Gruffudd Gryg's possibly misdirected salute to a tree at the abbey. Photographed c.1890

In spite of the hardships of the fourteenth century Dafydd ap Gwilym, the greatest of Welsh poets, and, above all, a wandering bard, found constant joy in nature, love and language. We might imagine him reclining in a sunny glade writing of skylarks, spring blossoms and achingly pretty girls, colouring his supple verse with the French words then seeping into Welsh. Although schooled in the official style of the court poets he launched a new poetry, pioneering a narrative and personal approach and creating the cywydd form with its seven-syllable lines of alliterative and chiming cynghanedd. The spirit of it is expressed in a translation by H. Idris Bell and David Bell.

A lover of song, I gathered and bound
The wealth of the cywydd in a bundle
of sound.

He loved nature in all its forms, birds, trees, snow and thunder. When he gazed at the night sky he pronounced:

A blessing on the Lord Creator's name
Who wrought the carpentry of the stars.

Born in Ceredigion around 1320, he travelled widely in Wales and often chanted his work to the accompaniment of a harp. He died around 1370 and his burial place is hotly disputed by his admirers to this day. He would smile, therefore, to know that he has two memorial stones, at the ruined abbeys of Talley in Carmarthenshire and Strata Florida, both lovely places.

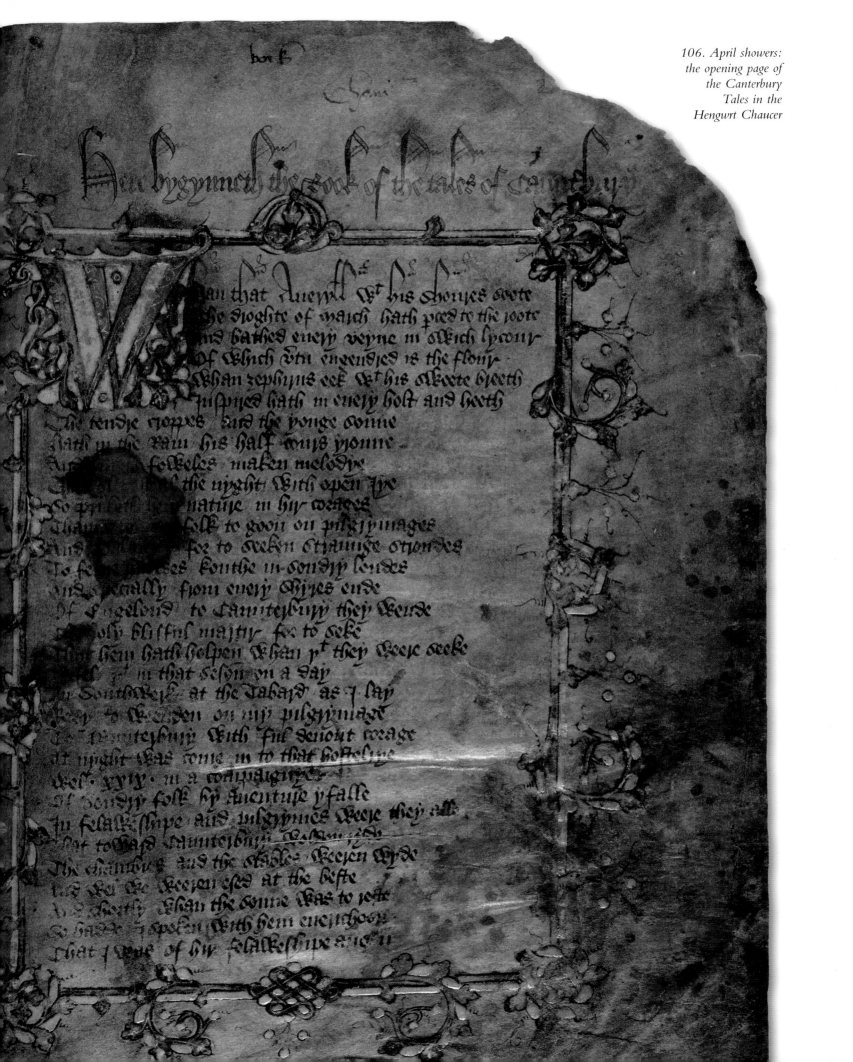

THE POET MERRY AND PROFOUND

A POCKETFUL OF PRAYERS

The twenty-four stories of the Canterbury Tales, Geoffrey Chaucer's greatest work, have been an entertainment for six centuries. The earliest-known text is one of the jewels of the National Library, its presence in Wales reflecting the interest that educated Welshmen took in English manuscripts from the Middle Ages onwards.

It belonged to a Chester draper in the 1550s and was probably in Caernarfon around the 1620s. Its famous sanctuary for more than two centuries was Robert Vaughan's library. Like Shakespeare, Chaucer wrote appealingly and accessibly for the crowd while remaining a writer of serious purpose in his comedy, his stories of love and the complexities of human life.

In medieval times devout worshippers consulted a book of hours to guide their personal prayers at home. If they were wealthy they had a private chapel for the purpose. But, wherever they knelt, the book of hours set the pattern for their devotions with its calendar of saints' days and prescriptions for prayers at regular times throughout the day. Many of the books were made for women, and the owners kept them close at hand, on a belt or tucked into a sleeve.

The Llanbeblig Book of Hours was compiled around 1390, a small book of 138 parchment pages, about six and a half inches high. A reference to the church of Saint Peblig links it with Caernarfon. Its remarkable features include pictures of God and the Holy Spirit; of Magnus Maximus, the Roman commander in Britain who appears in The Mabinogion as Macsen Wledig; and of the Virgin Mary with an unusual depiction of Christ crucified on a lily. The illustrations and fine lettering show us that the book was costly.

107. Daily devotions: (l to r)
The Llanbeblig Book of Hours, possibly owned by Isabella Godynough, d.1413
God the Holy Spirit;
Magnus Maximus;
The 'lily crucifixion'

*108. 'Thoughts of
more deep seclusion' –
William Wordsworth
was one of the poets
inspired by Tintern's
ruins. Tintern Abbey
Looking North. Louis
Haghe, 1855*

*109. Beautiful,
and not showy:
the Tintern Bible*

ULTRAVIOLET PROOF

The Cistercian order of monks, who took their name from Cîteaux in Burgundy, made a profound impact in Wales for their love of learning, simplicity and the breadth of their welcome to men of all kinds, rich or poor, educated or illiterate. The first Cistercians in Wales settled at Tintern in Monmouthshire. Their abbey, consecrated in 1288, fell into ruin after Henry VIII broke up the monasteries, but its soaring bare walls remain beautiful.

While it was being built, in the third quarter of the thirteenth century, the abbey acquired a Bible which today is in the National Library. It is a fine example of the hundreds of standard Bibles produced in the thirteenth century in response to the spread of literacy and university teaching. It is about nine and a half inches tall and its text, two columns to a page, was written by two scribes. The primary capital letters, in red and blue, are handsome but, in keeping with Cistercian taste, are not ostentatious. The Tintern Bible was not necessarily produced at Tintern. It may have been made in France. It was bound in the seventeenth century. The National Library bought it in 1988 for £30,000. A fifteenth-century inscription had been erased but was revealed by ultraviolet light, confirming that the Bible was a survivor of Tintern's medieval library.

110. Medieval
Astronomy:
Constellation
of Andromeda

Constellation
of Cassiopeia

Celestial sphere

STEERING
BY THE STARS

Long before men knew the continents and
seas they knew the heavens. The phases of
the sun, moon and stars were observable
certainties. Astronomy was the senior
science and navigation the first practical
application of it. The seafarer's need to find
his way across oceans by means of stars and
planets made navigation the chief scientific
quest for many centuries.

The National Library's oldest scientific
manuscript shows that astronomy was
long entangled in myth and astrology.
The Latin text, which includes descriptions
and diagrams of the constellations, is also
illustrated by zodiac images including Taurus
and Gemini. The manuscript's two sections
were written in the Limoges region of
France, one part around the year 1000
and the other in about 1150. It was in Plas
Power, in Denbighshire, for perhaps two
centuries before the National Library
bought it in 1913.

Constellation
of Serpentarius

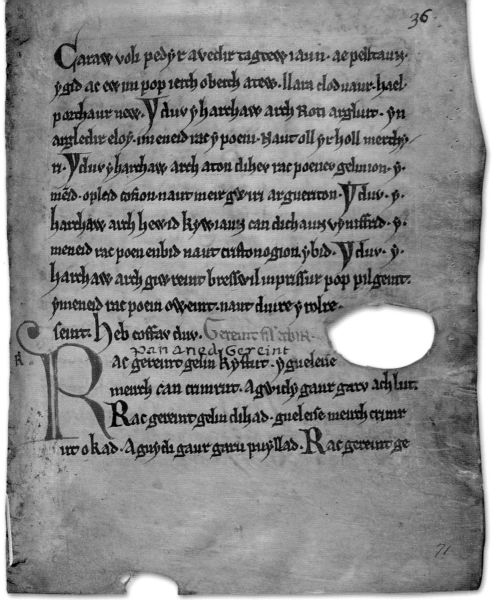

111. Writing
round the problem:
The Black Book
of Carmarthen

THE WORD IS OUT

Monastery scribes worked on parchment, the skins of sheep and goats soaked in lime and washed and relentlessly scraped until they were thin, supple and clean of fat. The name derives from the Turkish city of Pergamon where it originated. Calfskin parchment was called vellum, from the Latin for calf. Parchment often had the sort of imperfections that can be seen, for example, in The Black Book of Carmarthen, holes nibbled by parasites on the animal's

skin while it was still alive. Confronted by such imperfections the scribe who compiled the Black Book simply wrote around them.

Carbon ink could be erased. Permanent ink was made from iron sulphate, imported gum arabic, water, and from oak apples, the tumours created when the gall wasp lays its eggs in an oak leaf bud. Oak apples are rich in acid. Such 'iron ink' ate into parchment and was indelible, an important consideration for record keepers and makers of legal documents. But the balance of the mixture was critical. If it were too acidic it made holes.

Ancient Egyptians wrote on papyrus made from the pith of sedge or riverside grass. In the second century the Chinese made paper from hemp and pulped cloth dried on a frame. They kept the method secret for seven centuries until Arabs discovered it and took it to Spain. From there it spread slowly to France and England in the thirteenth and fourteenth centuries. Paper appeared in Wales around 1450. The invention of the printing press made its use universal.

A SONG FOR
SAINT DAVID

Officials ordered to search churches for religious books and papers banned under Henry VIII's Reformation were bloodhounds in human form. Little escaped them. Almost every document used in Catholic services was rooted out and burnt. But this is one of the rare survivors, no doubt carefully hidden in time of danger, the earliest-known music manuscript with a Welsh connection. It was written in the late fourteenth century and used in the diocese of Saint David's, the only known example of a full service written to celebrate Saint David's Day.

The chants were probably composed in the thirteenth century, evidence of the early use of music in Welsh churches. The music is antiphonic, meaning that two groups of singers chanted verses alternately, each responding to or echoing the other. The manuscript is known as the Penpont Antiphonal and was at Penpont in Breconshire during the 1550s.

112. Sacred notes:
Penpont Antiphonal

Owain Glyn Dŵr was about forty-six when he rose against English rule in September 1400. Intolerable English domination had made Welsh people feel alien in their own land. Glyn Dŵr was an attractive figure, a cultivated, lawyerly and hospitable squire, an experienced soldier who had fought for the English against the Scots.

In Shakespeare's perceptive portrayal he was a commanding and mysterious force, 'that great magician, damn'd Glendower.' Welsh people remember his vision of a future Wales with its own parliament, universities and church. Forever intrepid, Glyn Dŵr never submitted. He vanished from the mountains and died, perhaps in 1416, aged about sixty-two. His was the last revolt against English conquest. Detractors among the Welsh gentry disparaged him as a common rebel but, as a warrior, statesman and visionary he embodied the resilient mystique of an authentic and necessary national hero. His name rang down the years, the clang of a sword hammered on an anvil.

113. The battle won: Gruffudd Hiraethog's description of Glyn Dŵr's victory at Mynydd Hyddgen, 1401

114. Zodiac Man: the influence of the heavens on human health

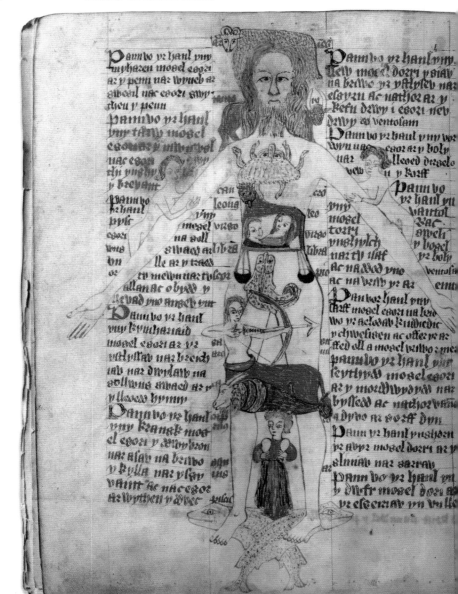

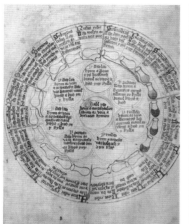

115. Testing the waters

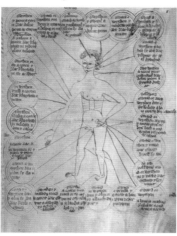

A measure of blood

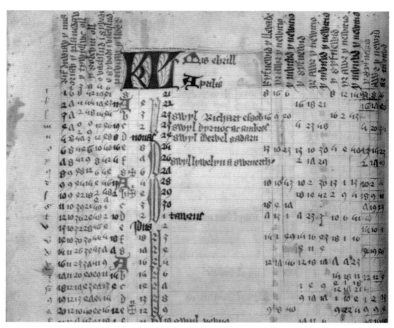

BLOODLINES

Playing the Welsh card was crucial in Henry Tudor's struggle for the English crown. Through his grandfather Owain Tudor he asserted descent from the ancient Welsh and British kings to support both his claim to the throne and his security after he had won it. For this reason he set up a commission in 1491 to investigate his grandfather's lineage and appointed Gutun Owain to it. Gutun was both the most knowledgeable genealogist of his time and a leading bardic figure. He also copied parts of the Black Book of Basingwerk. He was fascinated by medicine and astrology and in the 1490s compiled a remarkable illustrated book of medical information and instruction showing how the body should be bled to treat illness and how the varying colour of urine should be interpreted. His 'zodiac man' demonstrates astrological influences on the body.

POETIC LICENCE

Travelling poets were hired by great houses as entertainers, to compose elegies, wedding ditties and sumptuous verses of praise. At a time when wandering vagrants were looked on with suspicion and ran the risk of a whipping, poets needed proof that they were honest wordmongers. This document, below, issued by Lewys Morgannwg in the sixteenth century, vouched for the good character of a rhymer on the road.

116.

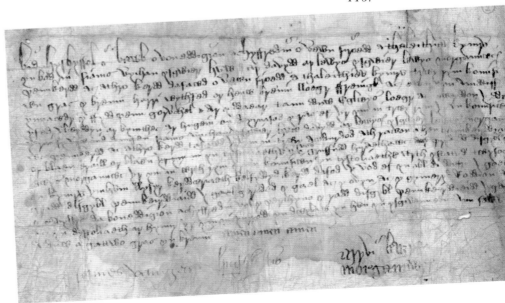

117. Welshmen spared: Henry IV's pardons granted in 1410 to Glyn Dŵr's supporters, including Jenkin ap Jenkin, Llewelyn ap Madog ap Llewelyn, Rys ap David ap Howel, Madog ap Ieuan ap Madog

NAMING WALES

In their kin-based rural societies long ago the Welsh knew exactly who they were. Their names attested to their ancestry and identity, important in determining inheritance and social status. A man typically carried his father's, grandfather's and perhaps great-grandfather's name, each joined by ap, from mab, meaning son of. Hence the bailiff of Llanfyllin in 1585: Cadwaladr ap David ap John ap Huw ap Moris.

After the Act of Union, which made English the sole language of government in Wales, officials insisted on surnames in the English fashion. The church, too, demanded settled names in baptismal registers. The Welsh gentry readily adopted the English custom. Thomas ap Richard ap Hywel ap Ieuan of Mostyn was told to take the surname Mostyn – 'one name, like a Christian.' The dynasty of Henry VII, Henry VIII and Elizabeth I bore the name of Tudor because their Welsh ancestor, when taking a surname, chose his grandfather's name, Tudor, rather than his father's, Maredudd.

In the long renaming of Wales surnames were shaped by use and the mishearing of English clerks. Hence Ifan ab Ifan became Evan Evans. Often the ap/ab melted into the new name, as in Evan Bevan. Tomos ap Hywel became Thomas Howells or Thomas Powell. The relatively small pool of baptismal names, such as William, Robert, Thomas and Edward, ensured a corresponding paucity of surnames. John was rendered into Jones, although there was no j in Welsh; and as John in various forms was the most popular given name it became, as Jones, the most common surname. A Victorian Registrar General concluded: 'John Jones is in Wales a perpetual incognito.' In reality both the forenames and surnames of Wales are marks of Welsh distinctiveness.

AN IMPROVING BOOK

Sir John Price, the civil servant who rescued The Black Book of Carmarthen, believed the printing press was God's gift and that a book in Welsh was vital for his countrymen's spiritual good. In 1546 he wrote and published the first volume printed in Welsh. It was probably produced in London. The only complete copy of it is in the National Library. It was untitled and took its name from its opening words, Yny lhyvyr hwnn: In this book.

Its contents included the Welsh alphabet, a calendar, agricultural advice, the Lord's Prayer, the ten commandments and lists of the seven deadly sins and seven virtues. Sir John was an Oxford-educated lawyer, an MP and landowner. As chief registrar of the Crown in ecclesiastical matters he was an active official in the dissolution of the monasteries. His successful life was said to have been 'like a long summer's day.'

118. Yny lhyvyr hwnn,
1546: title page

MORGAN'S MISSION

At the end of 1587 the Reverend
William Morgan packed his satchels at
his Denbighshire vicarage and set off on
horseback for London, 200 miles distant.
The bags held the great work of his life,
the bundled manuscript of his Welsh Bible.
With the help of some friends he had
spent ten years translating the Old and
New Testaments from Greek and Hebrew,
languages he had studied at Cambridge
university. We can imagine him dismounting
at an inn after a day's weary ride along the
bony roads, unloading his precious bags,
thankful not to have met a highwayman.

In London he stayed with Gabriel
Goodman, dean of Westminster, an old
Cambridge friend, and every day went
to George Bishop's press in Saint Paul's
churchyard to supervise the printing of the
Bible. He himself did the vital work of proof-
correcting. London printers made numerous
errors in their grappling with the unfamiliar
Welsh language. At last, in September 1588,
the first edition of a thousand copies was
published by Christopher Barker, the
Queen's printer. Each leather-bound
Bible contained 1,122 pages of French
paper printed with French ink.

John Whitgift, archbishop
of Canterbury, helped to finance
the translation, fearing that without
it Wales was vulnerable to Catholic
influence. He ordered Welsh bishops
to get it into their churches by Christmas;
and the thick volumes were despatched on
horseback to Wales. At one pound a copy
they were far beyond the ordinary pocket,
but Thomas Jones, a parson, was so moved
by Morgan's language that he urged
Welshmen to sell their shirts to buy a
copy: 'Dos, gwerth dy bais, y Cymro.'
In the twentieth century R.S. Thomas
praised its 'passages of serene prose.'

Morgan burned with a strong sense of
mission. He insisted that 'unless religion
be taught in the common tongue it will
be unknown.' His work made him the most
significant Reformation figure in Wales and
placed Welsh in the company of French,
German, English and Spanish as a Bible
language. It made Welsh count, an emblem
of Welsh nationality, and saved the language
from fragmenting into disparate dialects.
Revised in 1620, it was the authorized
Welsh version until the translation of 1988.

Morgan was born in 1545 at Tŷ Mawr,
near Penmachno, and schooled by local
teachers before going to Saint John's,
Cambridge. He was priest at Llanbadarn
Fawr near Aberystwyth, Welshpool, Denbigh
and Llanrhaeadr-ym-Mochnant, and bishop
of Llandaff and of Saint Asaph. He worked
on his Bible against a background of torment,
the abuse and writs of a discontented
neighbour. He died in 1604, leaving £110,
a saddle, two peacocks and two swans.

*119. The first
Book of Moses
in the 1588 Bible*

*120. The great
achievement: the title
page of Morgan's Bible*

Y BEIBL CYS-
SEGR-LAN. SEF
YR HEN DESTA-
MENT, A'R NEWYDD.

2. Timoth. 3. 14, 15.

Eithr aros di yn y pethau a ddyscaist, ac a ymddyried-
wydi ti, gan wybod gan bwy y dyscaist.
Ac i ti eryn fachgen wybod yr scrythur lân, yr hon
sydd abl i'th wneuthur yn ddoeth i iechydwria-
eth, trwy'r ffydd yr hon sydd yng-Hrist Iesu.

Imprinted at London by the Deputies of
CHRISTOPHER BARKER,
Printer to the Queenes most excel-
lent Maiestie.

1588.

PENNED IN PRISON

As a master copyist John Jones made a remarkable contribution to Welsh literature. He spent more than twelve years in jail for debt and his cell was his studio. His penmanship made his copies works of art in their own right. Born in 1585 at Gellilyfdy, Flintshire, he was a lawyer and an associate of Robert Vaughan who collected more than a hundred of his manuscripts, now in the National Library. When Jones died in the Fleet prison in London in 1658 Vaughan recovered copied work from his cell.

THE COLLECTOR

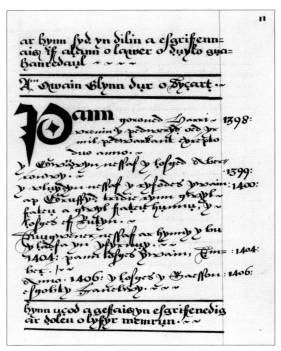

121. The hand of John Jones, Gellilyfdy:
a copy of an account of the burning of
Ruthin by Owain Glyn Dŵr's forces

One of the greatest of collectors, Robert Vaughan, 1592–1667, built a bridge from the past to the future, the beginnings of a National Library. At Hengwrt, his manor house near Dolgellau in Merioneth, he gathered more than half of the 250 medieval Welsh books which survive today including The Black Book of Carmarthen, the Hendregadredd Manuscript, The White Book of Rhydderch, the Book of Taliesin, the Laws of Hywel Dda and the Chronicle of the Princes. Vaughan was an Oxford-educated squire who learnt history and genealogy from bards who gave him old manuscripts. He was a skilled copyist. He said his collecting was driven by 'love of my country and our ancestors.'

122. Robert Vaughan's
own catalogue of his
library at Hengwrt

In the latter years of Queen Elizabeth's reign fewer than a thousand Catholics were counted in Wales. Some worked secretly to keep their faith alive. One of them, the undercover missionary Robert Gwyn, born near Pwllheli, was probably the author of Y Drych Cristianogawl, the Christian Mirror, the first book printed in Wales.

It was a dramatic story. Seven Catholic activists set up a press in a cave in the Little Orme at Llandudno in 1586-87 and printed Gwyn's book, giving it a Rouen imprint and the false date of 1585 to mislead government agents. Nevertheless officials heard about the cave and the printers fled. One of the fugitives, William Davies, was arrested and executed at Beaumaris in 1593 by authorities fearful of Catholic influence. The only complete text of Gwyn's cave book survives in the National Library.

123. Dangerous words: men risked their lives to print this book. It dealt with Catholic teaching on The Four Last Things: Death, The Day of Judgment, Hell and Heaven.

Y DRYCH CRISTIA NOGAWL:

YN YR HWN Y DICHON POB CRISTIAWN GANFOD GWREIDHIN A DECHREVAD pob daioni fprydawl:

SEF GWYBOD MODH I WASANA ethu Duw, drwy ei garu ai ofni yn fwy na dim, ag i daflu ymaith beth bynnag a r a fo rwyftr i hynny.

Y RHANN GYNTAF yn peri gwafanaethu Duw drwy ei garu.

Conuertimini ad me, & conuertar ad vos, ait Dominus exercituum.3.Malach.7.

Dymchwelwch chwi ataw fi, a mineu a dhymchwelaf ataw chwitheu, med Arglwyd y lhuoed.

Rhotomagi apud hæredes Iathroi Fauonis.

1585

THE SHAPE OF WALES

Modern cartography began in 1477 when scholars reconstructed maps first drawn in the second century by the astronomer Ptolemy of Alexandria. Although they were the vision of a man who had been dead for 1,300 years they were nevertheless an influential idea of what the world looked like. In 1569 Gerardus Mercator illustrated a cartographic volume with a figure of Atlas bearing the world on his shoulders, and thereafter any book of maps was an atlas.

Demand for maps and mariners' charts flourished during the boom in trade and exploration in the sixteenth century. The first great map of Wales was made by Humphrey Llwyd of Denbigh, on a scale of one inch to eight and one-fifth miles. Embellished with a sea monster, it was engraved by Abraham Ortelius in Antwerp in 1573 and reprinted many

times. Christopher Saxton's survey produced excellent maps of Wales in the 1570s and these influenced John Speed whose map of 1611 set new standards of accuracy.

In 1737 Lewis Morris, a self-taught surveyor, who worked as a customs officer in Anglesey, began a coastal survey of Wales in response to seafarers' complaints that inadequate charts caused shipwrecks. His work took eleven years and he published a chart of the coast from Llandudno to Milford Haven and plans of twenty-five harbours, a significant contribution to safer navigation. His son William extended the chart in 1800 to cover the entire coast. Lewis Morris and his brother Richard founded the Honourable Society of Cymmrodorion as a focus for Welsh intellectual life in London.

124.
Saving life at sea: title-page of Lewis Morris's pioneering plans of harbours, bars, bays and roads in St. George's Channel, 1748

126. Right: Christopher Saxton's map of 1580 clearly delineated the border of Wales

125. Safe haven: Cardigan Bay bar and harbour

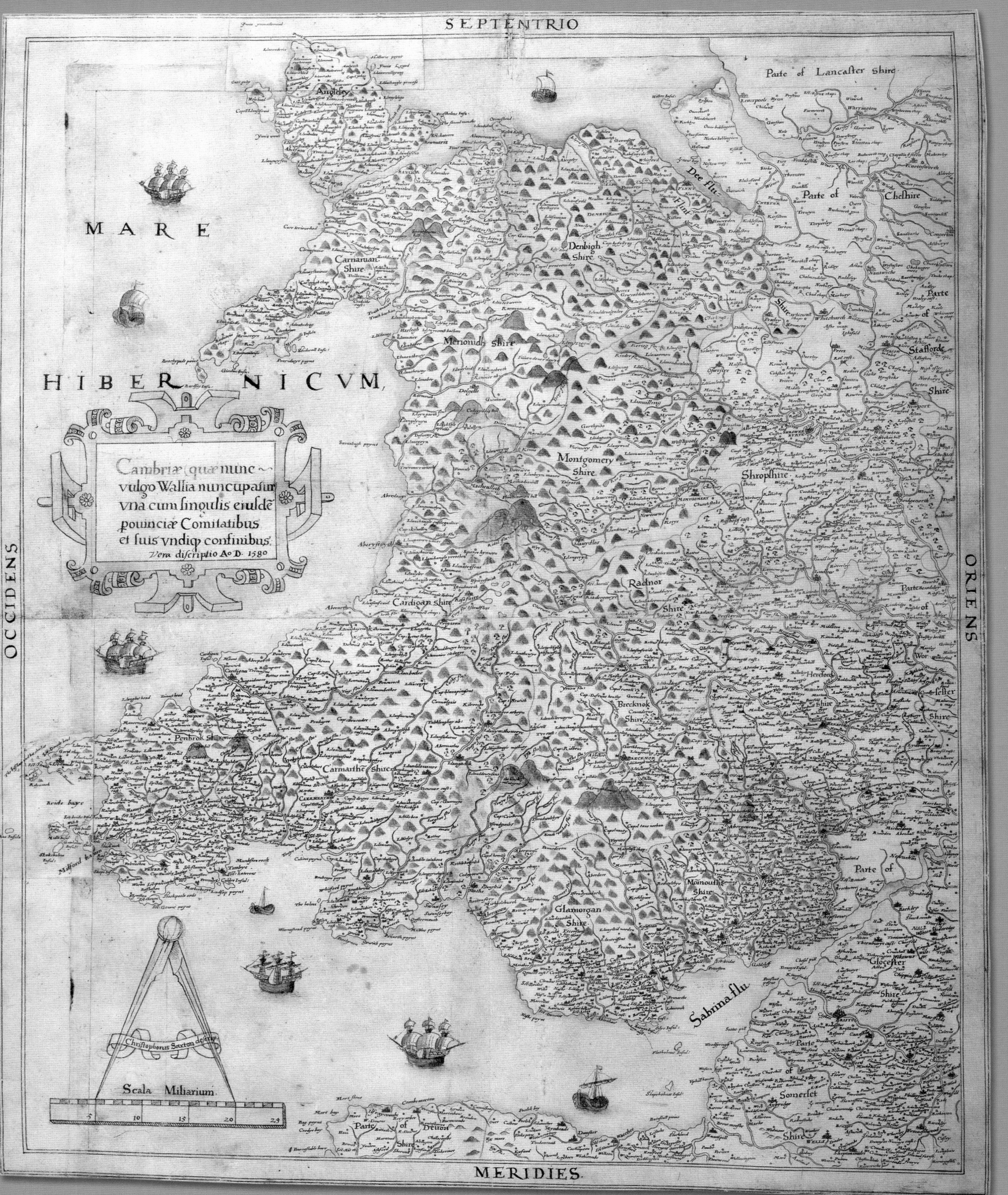

SEPTENTRIO

OCCIDENS

ORIENS

MERIDIES.

MARE

HIBER NICVM,

Cambria, (quae nunc
vulgo Wallia nuncupatur)
vna cum singulis eiusde
pouinciae Comitatibus,
et suis vndiq confinibus.
Vera discriptio A° D. 1580

Scala Miliarium.

5   10   15   20   25

Christophorus Saxton descrip.

Parte of Lancaster shire

Parte of Chelhire

Parte of Stafforde Shire

Anglesey

Carnaruan Shire

Merionidh Shire

Denbigh Shire

Dee flu.

Montgomery Shire

Shroplhire

Cardigan shire

Radnor Shire

Penbrok Sh.

Carmarthe Shiere

Brecknok Shire

Hereford Shire

Wor... shire

Glamorgan Shire

Monouth Shire

Sabrina flu.

Glocester Shire

Parte of Somerset Shire

Parte of Deuen Shire

BRIEF ENCOUNTER

Dick Turpin and his fellow highwaymen on the English roads notoriously shouted 'Stand and deliver!' when they stopped and robbed stagecoaches. Passengers on a coach in Glamorgan in 1755 heard the chilling command: 'Sefwch, God dammoch chwi, efe ceiswch arian chwi', translated in the record of the highwaymen's trial as 'Stand, God damn you, I want your money.' The passengers boldly refused and the robbers bolted. They were later captured and transported for seven years.

127. Banished to the ends of the earth: court authority for transporting John Jones, convicted of fraud in 1790

128. Highwaymen indicted

SHAKESPEARE'S SIREN

As charmers of sailors mermaids appeared in stories in many cultures from ancient times. Belief in their existence, as well as reported sightings, persisted into the eighteenth century. No doubt seamen catching sight of a manatee, an ocean mammal, holding its young to its breast with a flipper, thought they were seeing a mermaid. And perhaps the cries of seals sounded human to men long at sea. Wales has its share of mermaid sightings. This pamphlet tells how Thomas Raynold and others kept watch on 'a mermaid' at Pendine, Carmarthenshire, in 1603. There was a ready appetite for such intriguing tales. Shakespeare used the word mermaid as a euphemism for a courtesan.

THE SMUGGLER'S TALE

In Carmarthen jail, awaiting execution for murder, thirty-year-old William Owen wrote the story of his adventurous criminal life. Born at Nevern in Pembrokeshire he became a smuggler in British and Caribbean waters. He was cleared of killing a customs officer at Cardigan in 1744 and returned to smuggling. But in 1747 he was convicted of murdering another smuggler at Cardigan.

Memoirs like Owen's are extremely rare. His story, purchased by the National Library in 1982, is valuable because it includes a transcript of his trial at Carmarthen, the only known transcript of eighteenth-century criminal proceedings in Wales. Owen gave his life story to the Carmarthen jailer, probably in payment for decent food in the days before his execution.

130. Exclusive: My life of crime by a notorious smuggler

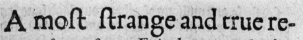

129. Fantasy girl: A most strange and true report of a monsterous fish

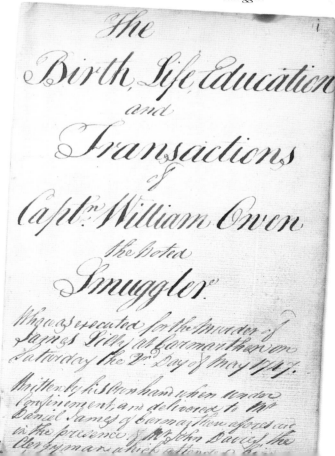

READ ALL ABOUT IT

Almanacs were the popular reading of their day, cheap paperbacks sold by pedlars and filled with ballads, sailors' farewells, verses, weather lore, calendars, dates of fairs and accounts of murders, mine accidents and shipwrecks. They were poorly printed and few have survived, but for scholars they are fascinating sources of slang and colloquial usage.

Almanac compilers held eisteddfodau in taverns, keeping alive the traditions of poetry and songs. The first almanac in Welsh was published in 1681 by Thomas Jones of Shrewsbury, but it was not until 1733 that almanacs were published in Wales itself, flourishing first in north Wales and steadily seeping into the south. They stimulated and responded to a popular appetite for illustrations. Almanac woodcuts were commonly stuck to the walls of cottages. Penny almanacs published by Hughes of Wrexham sold 60,000 copies a year in the 1870s. Their mixture of useful information, sentimental songs and stories of love, crime and punishment set a pattern for the Victorian popular papers which supplanted them.

131.

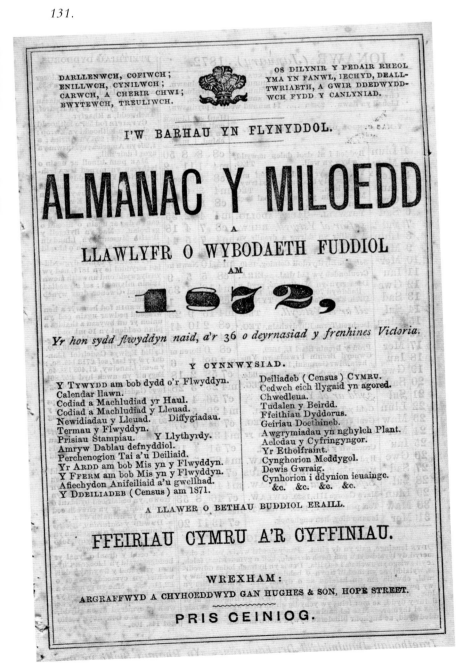

A PREACHER
IN A PEAR TREE

Howel Harris was thirty in 1744 when he applied for a licence to marry Anne Williams, of Erwood, Brecon. Her father, a local squire, opposed the match and raised a legal objection. From a window of her father's home Anne climbed down a pear tree and into the waiting arms of Harris, her Romeo. The couple applied to the bishop's court at Brecon and won permission to marry.

COMMANDOS OF THE WORD

Their minds afire, Howel Harris, Daniel Rowland and William Williams formed an evangelical commando in the spread of Methodism in eighteenth-century Wales. Harris was the formidable organizing genius, Rowland the spellbinding pulpiteer, Williams the prodigious author of hymns. They were determined to save every Welsh soul and preached the stark choice of conversion or hellfire.

It was a time of religious effervescence throughout the Protestant world both in Europe and America. Harris, born in 1714, started evangelizing in his native Breconshire in 1735. Uncompromising and dictatorial, he rode hard, preached hard and suffered the attacks of ruffians who were often encouraged in this violence by squires and Anglican clergymen. During his lifetime

north Wales resisted Methodist missionaries. In 1737 he joined forces with Rowland, a curate who, like Harris, put the fear of the devil into his listeners. Crowds who flocked to their open-air performances were called Jumpers for the way they leapt and shouted in sensuous joy.

Harris and Rowland were driven apart by their clashing egos and doctrinal differences. The movement split. Harris's wife and supporters were dismayed by his relationship with Madam Sidney Griffith, the travelling companion he believed was a prophetess. She funded the self-sufficient farming and craft commune of 120 converts he established at Trefeca in Talgarth, near Brecon. When war broke out with France he became a militia officer and recruiter in what he saw as a religious struggle against a Catholic regime.

His disciple, the Countess of Huntingdon, shocked her aristocratic friends by founding a Methodist college at Trefeca. Harris taught there and meanwhile wrote prolifically. His 290 diary volumes, a valuable source of information about his times, are in the National Library. Thanks to the peacemaking of William Williams, Howel Harris and Daniel Rowland patched their differences in the 1760s. Rowland built the chapel at Llangeitho, Cardiganshire, which became the focus of Welsh Methodism. Harris died in 1773 after nearly forty turbulent years of preaching. Twenty thousand people attended his funeral.

*132. Firm-jawed
and fearless:
Howel Harris*

THE SWEET SINGER

William Williams was born in 1717 and had a classical education. At the age of twenty he went to hear Howel Harris speak at Talgarth and declared that he 'heard the voice of heaven.' In time he succeeded Harris as the Methodist movement's organizer. He was not a compelling preacher in the Harris and Rowland mould, nor, like them, a tempestuous personality. He moved crowds in a different way, as the passionate poet of the awakening, the most stirring of hymn-writers. The hundreds of hymns he composed became a characteristic of Wales itself. Most of the songs in the hymn book were his, marked by a simple W beside each one.

Although his unorthodox writing did not follow literary traditions he had a genius for expressing love and wonder with moving simplicity. He reached the heart with his vision of Christian life. And he advised that composers should only write hymns if they felt 'breathed upon by the breezes of the Holy Spirit.' He was one of the great poets of Wales and a significant prose-writer. He was also a tireless travelling preacher.

133. Hymnody house:
Pantycelyn farm, in a secluded valley
on the edge of the Epynt hills, c.1925

134. Inspirational:
the stream of poetry

He became known by the sobriquet of Pantycelyn, the name of his mother's farm in Carmarthenshire, where he and his wife had eight children and lived comfortably on his earnings as farmer, publisher and astute businessman. He died in 1791.

135. Straight backs: William Williams and his imposing chair which is now in the nation's library

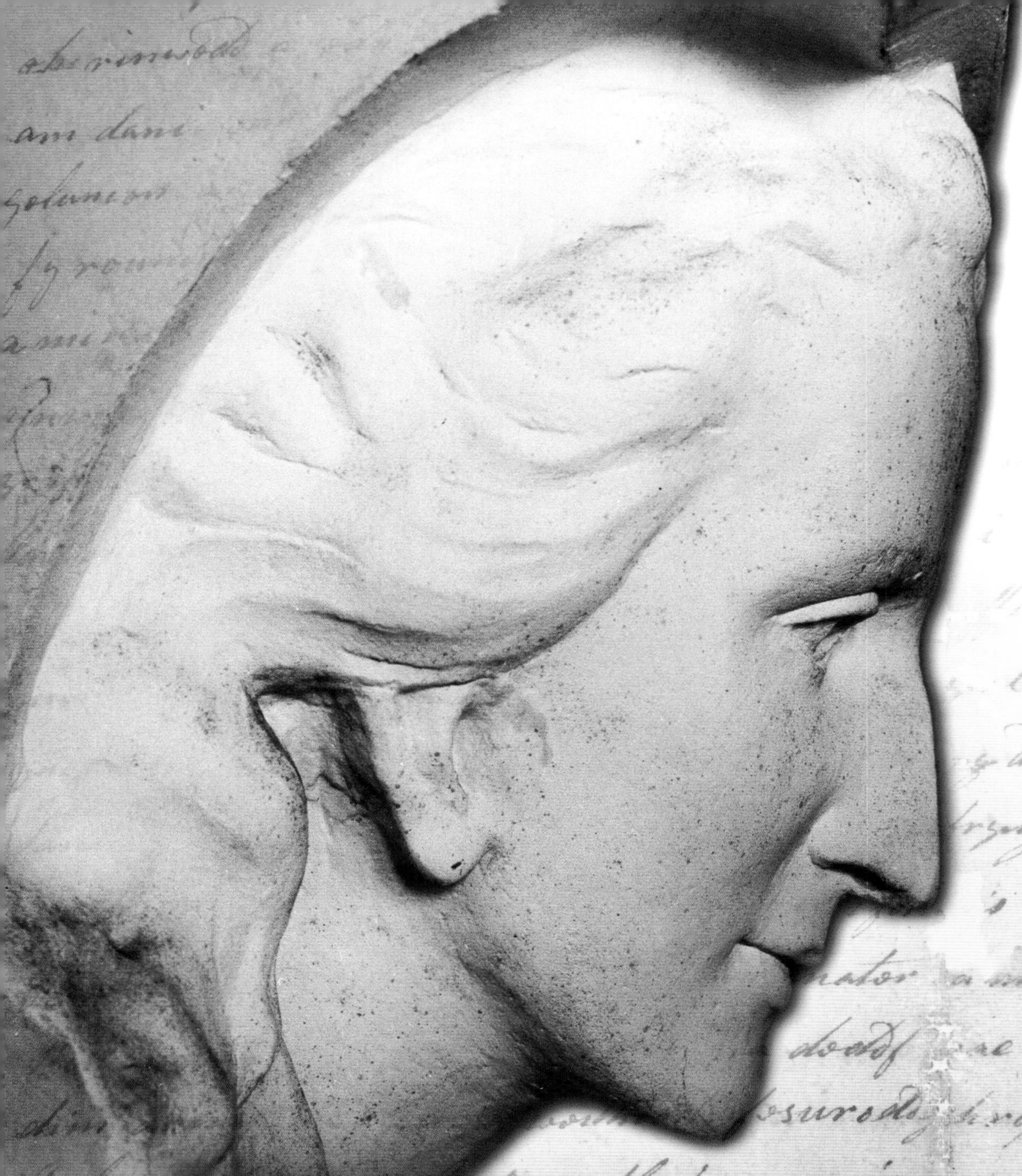

136. Left:
Intensity of feeling and
mysterious knowledge:
Ann Griffiths, from
a bas relief as seen in
Dolanog Memorial
Chapel. Only
seventy-four of
her verses survive

137. Below:
A letter she
wrote to her friend
Elizabeth Evans

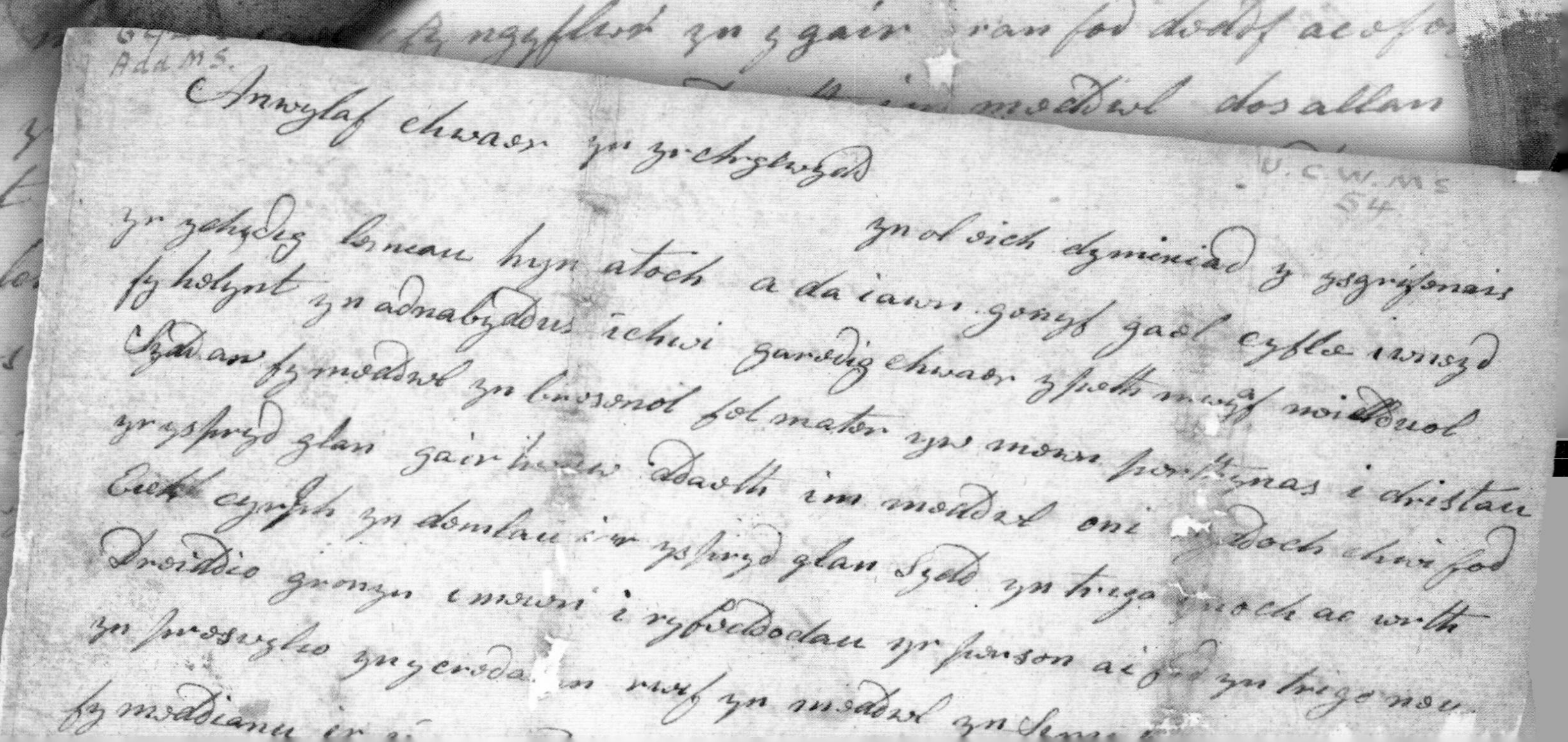

A GIRL BATHED IN LIGHT

Nineteen-year-old Ann Griffiths, who loved to dance and sing, experienced a religious awakening while listening to a sermon. She gave herself to Methodism and for the remaining ten years of her life expressed her passion in the poetry of her hymns. She is considered one of Europe's leading religious poets, part of the great Methodist hymn-writing wave of the early eighteenth century.

She committed little to paper and recited her ecstatic verses to her illiterate maidservant Ruth Evans who memorized them. Ann, born in 1776, married a farmer in 1804 and died the following year shortly after bearing a daughter who also died. Ruth married a preacher, John Hughes of Pontrobert, and recalled Ann's hymns as he wrote them down. A letter in Ann's hand survives in the National Library. She lived all her life at Dolwar-fach, a Montgomeryshire hill farm, and to this day it is a place of Methodist pilgrimage. Dr Rowan Williams, archbishop of Canterbury, used his own translation of one of her hymns in his enthronement service in 2003.

A PULPIT GIANT

138. Celebrity: Christmas Evans, William Roos, c.1835

With his commanding presence, his single protruding eye and dramatic style, Christmas Evans was a celebrated performer in the nineteenth-century heroic age of travelling preachers. To one of those who heard him he seemed to glow like a volcano, 'casting out his lava like a seething river over his listeners until all their emotions were aroused.'

Born on Christmas Day 1776 he was illiterate until he was seventeen, and then, so it was said, learnt to read the Welsh Bible in a month. He preached to Baptist congregations in Anglesey from 1791 to 1826 and was later a minister in Caerphilly, Cardiff and Caernarfon. His legendary sermons filled chapels and hillsides, gathering followers for the faith and gifts of money for the chapel-building frenzy of his time.

GO YE THEREFORE AND TEACH

Missionaries from Wales were heroes to the chapel congregations who sent them to spread the gospel in Africa, India, China, the Pacific, the Caribbean, Korea and elsewhere. John Davies, a spiritual influence on Ann Griffiths, sailed for Tahiti in 1800 and spent fifty-four years there. Remembered as John Davies Tahiti he compiled a Tahitian grammar and translated The Pilgrim's Progress and parts of the Bible. Letters he wrote to John Hughes of Pontrobert are in the National Library.

Equally famous was Thomas Jones, a Montgomeryshire miller, who in 1841 began to evangelize among the people of the rain-sodden Khasi hills of north-eastern India. The first to write down the local language, he translated scriptures and Matthew's gospel and composed hymns.

His troubles multiplied tragically. His wife died in 1845. His subsequent marriage to a fifteen-year-old English girl and disagreements with other missionaries led to expulsion from the church. He was chased out of the hills by a ruthless trader and died in Calcutta in 1849. His name is still revered. Welsh missionaries worked in the Khasi hills for 128 years, leaving a legacy of schools, hospitals, Welsh hymns and the Khasi national anthem sung to the tune of Hen Wlad fy Nhadau.

Accounts of missionary work were popular in Welsh newspapers in Victorian times and promoted pride and a sense of involvement in imperial progress and the struggle against a perceived heathenism. Increasingly, this romantic view was questioned, and sceptics began to see missionaries as players in Victorian colonial expansion.

139. Tales of the South Pacific: John Davies writing home to John Hughes, Pontrobert, in 1842

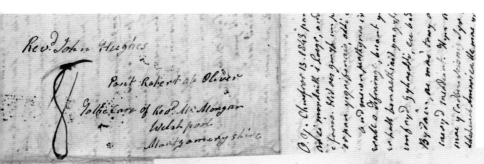

A RAINBOW MADE OF STONE

The bridge over the Taff at Pontypridd, famous for its daring and elegance, was built in 1756 by William Edwards, a self-taught stonemason and engineering genius. With an arch of 140 feet it was in its day the longest single span bridge in the world, longer even than the celebrated Rialto in Venice, and is still regarded as a significant pioneering work.

Edwards was commissioned to build the bridge to connect two country estates. It took him ten years of trial and error. His first three efforts collapsed into the surging river but he learnt from each failure. When at last the construction was finished an article in the influential Gentleman's Magazine drew attention to this 'very remarkable bridge' and writers, artists and tourists flocked to see it. A poet declared it would stand 'to the day of judgement.' Richard Wilson, the first of many artists who celebrated it, depicted a slender and

soaring span uniting two parts of a picturesque landscape, a symbol of the Romantic age. Its image appeared on ceramics, Nantgarw pottery ware and the dinner service of Catherine the Great of Russia. The bridge gave birth to the village of Newbridge which grew up around it. In 1856 it changed its name to Pontypridd to avoid confusion with other Newbridges. On badges and crests the bridge is Pontypridd's celebrated emblem. William Edwards later designed the new town at Morriston, near Swansea.

He was moved by the passion of Howel Harris to become a Methodist, later an Independent, and, ordained in 1745, grew into a preacher of renown. As his memorial at Groes-wen chapel, near Caerphilly, says, he was 'a builder for both worlds.'

140. The Great Bridge over the Taaffe. Richard Wilson, 1775

THE GREAT BRIDGE OVER THE TAAFFE. — LE GRAND PONT SUR LA TAAFFE.
in South Wales. dans la Principauté de Galles.

COPPER BOTTOMED GUARANTEE

European seafarers venturing into the oceans in sailing ships soon met a dangerous enemy: the teredo. They called it a worm, but it was a form of warm-water clam that bored into ships' timbers and riddled them with holes. It thrived in the Caribbean and along the American coast. Seamen tried to protect ships' hulls with coats of pitch, tallow and sulphur, even brown paper.

But the only effective defence against the ship-eating teredo was to sheath hulls with thin copper sheets. These also inhibited the growth of weed that made ships slow. Captains begged the Admiralty to provide them with copper-bottomed vessels to defeat both the teredo and the French. Much of the copper was supplied from the Anglesey mine run by Thomas Williams, a local solicitor. His business skill and great wealth earned him the title of 'the Copper King.' The copper ore was gouged out by hand and hammered by hundreds of men, women and children into small pieces for smelting. It was gruelling work. But Thomas Williams, who died in 1802, was affectionately remembered in Anglesey as Twm Chwarae Teg, Tom Fair Play.

141. Amlwch: the Anglesey copper trade made it a thriving port in the eighteenth and nineteenth centuries. William Daniell, 1813

142. Gentry splendour: Plas Teg 'A Tour in Wales'

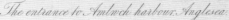
The entrance to Amlwch harbour, Anglesea.

143. Ruined splendour: Denbigh 'A Tour in Wales'

TRAVELLING MAN

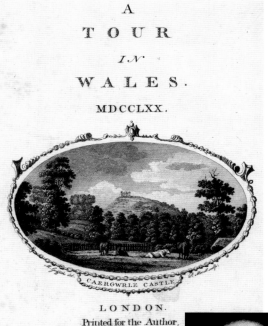

For many years visitors saw the Welsh landscape as wild and fearsome. But from the middle of the eighteenth century writers and artists decided it was wild and wonderful. War in Europe curtailed tours to France and Italy, and Wales became a fashionable alternative. New roads, stagecoaches and hotels made it more accessible. Wordsworth, Coleridge, Shelley and others came to write, and painters created a demand for Welsh scenes. In his book on the Wye in 1782 the English writer William Gilpin framed rules for observing landscape and started the cult of the picturesque.

The most influential of many books describing the country was Thomas Pennant's Tours in Wales, published in 1778, 1781 and 1783. It covered only the six northern counties. Pennant was an anglicized Flintshire squire who looked around him and loved what he saw: the countryside and history of Wales. He was a realist, not a romantic, and much preferred science and fact to airy legends. To his writing he brought the skills of a renowned naturalist, geologist, zoologist and inquisitive collector. He was genial and persuasive with a large network of learned contacts, and certainly the best Welsh travel author of his time, thorough and a master of detail. He loved his horseback journeys and had plenty of money to finance his trips in Scotland, Cornwall, Ireland and Wales.

Pennant was picture-minded and in 1769 discovered and hired the untrained but talented artist Moses Griffith to illustrate his books. Griffith worked for Pennant and his son for fifty years and was busily employed. As Pennant wrote to a friend: 'I would most cheerfully permit Moses to copy for you; but I give you my word his time is so fully taken up that he has not a moment's leisure.' Writer and illustrator travelled as a team, first to Scotland, then through north Wales. Griffith's outstanding work was the series of original paintings he did for twelve special large copies of A Tour in Wales. The two surviving volumes are in the National Library.

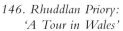

145. Self portrait by Moses Griffith 1747–1819

Pennant knew little Welsh and was helped by his friend John Lloyd of Caerwys to compose a moving account of the life of 'our chieftain' Owain Glyn Dŵr, a rediscovery that led to Glyn Dŵr becoming the national hero. Pennant was a friend of the naturalist Sir Joseph Banks who sailed with Captain James Cook. Cook gave the name New Wales to the east coast of Australia, a proposal Banks supported, knowing it would please his friend in Wales. Pennant, born 1726, died in 1798 at his birthplace and home in Downing.

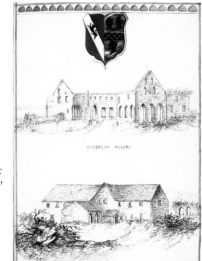

146. Rhuddlan Priory: 'A Tour in Wales'

THE BATTLE OF BANGOR

147. Poking fun: Welsh rarebit is thrown at the bishop of Bangor in an election row, 1796

CHEESE AND RED HERRINGS

From the seventeenth century English caricaturists drew readily-recognized stereotypes of Wales and the Welsh. They mounted them on goats, furnished them with harps and often called them Taffy, a corruption of Dafydd. They stuck leeks in their hats, armed them with upside-down swords and supplied them with the cheese and smoked herrings, known as red herrings, that were thought to be their favourite food. The goat-riding character Shon ap Morgan, who appeared in illustrations of the seventeenth and eighteenth centuries, was said to have died after a Saint David's day feast of 'leeks, sheese and red herrings.'

Readers were endlessly entertained by ridicule of the supposed Welsh pronunciation of English, by the Welsh patronymic with its linking string of aps, and by insulting comments about Welsh women. The Welshman of woodcut cartoons and engravings was typically poor but also hot-blooded and stubborn.

Caricaturists also jeered at the Prince of Wales, who was not at all Welsh, by showing him on a saddled goat. A cartoon of 1786 entitled Taffy and Hur wife, Shentleman of Wales, depicted the prince and his garter-revealing mistress, Mrs Fitzherbert, grotesquely astride a goat. As butts of English humour and prejudice the Welsh preceded the Irish and Scots.

148. Shon-ap-Morgan, Shentleman c.1747

*149. A Welch
Tandem. James
Gillray, 1801*

*150.
Spitted:
Sir Watkin
Williams Wynn
lampooned, 1745*

*151. A glimpse of stocking, something shocking:
a cartoonist's jibe in 1786 at the Prince of Wales, later George IV*

Noble purpose drove Edward Williams. He wanted his countrymen to feel a pride in their story. He knew that, living cheek by jowl with a powerful neighbour in a rapidly-changing world, they longed for assurance that they counted for something. So he gave them a place at the table, a sustaining myth and pageantry, complete with heroes, poets and sacred places, a visionary and inspiring version of their history.

152.
The stonemason's price list, 1779

Edward Williams, jun.
MARBLE-MASON,
AT
Flimſton, near Cowbridge ;

MAKES all Sorts of *Chimney-pieces, Monuments, Tombs, Head-ſtones,* and every other Article in the MARBLE and FREESTONE-MASONRY, in the neweſt and neat-eſt Manner, and on the moſt reaſonable Terms.

As he has for many Years regularly followed *LONDON* and other capital Towns under the b hopes he will be found capable of executing any of cles to the Satisfaction of all who may be pleaſed to their Commands, and on cheaper Terms than th th Trade without ever having followed it where Knowledge of it could be acquired.

As there are various Sorts of good *Marble* found of GLAMORGAN, *Monuments, Tables, Chimney pieces,* had very cheap.

Marble Tables, Chimney pieces, &c. clean'd and n reaſonable Terms ; alſo Letters cut on old *Monume*

Orders directed to him at *Flimſton*, or at the *Pr* to Mr. *Bradley*, at the *Horſe and Jockey,* in *Cowbrid* attended to.

R. THOMAS, PRINTER, COWBRIDGE, 1

The bardic name he adopted, Iolo Morganwg, Iolo of Glamorgan, reflected his devotion to his native county. He was born at Llancarfan in 1747, a stonemason's son, and learnt his father's craft. He had no formal schooling but he emerged as a self-taught historian, naturalist and authority on Welsh literature, language and music. He studied manuscripts in the libraries of the Glamorgan gentry and was, significantly, an indefatigable and observant walker and note-scribbler. Little escaped his eye. He seemed to possess the intellect and energy of half a dozen.

In London, where he sought work as a stonemason, his interest in literature blossomed into his passion. He shone as a star of the London Welsh, arguing about history and literature, and was meanwhile drawn to democratic and radical ideas of

153. *The great observer: Iolo Morganwg.*
Robert Cruikshank from Recollections
and Anecdotes of Edward Williams

IOLO MORGANWG, A PERSONAL RECOLLECTION.

the American and French revolutions. He saw Welsh history flowing unbroken from antiquity and claimed he had been entrusted with the secrets of the druids, the heroic teachers and priests of ancient Britain. He invented a convocation of druids in London in 1792, and at Carmarthen in 1819 transplanted it into the eisteddfod as a permanent ornament.

Increasingly he fabricated documents in support of a glorious Welsh past, his forgeries running from minor enhancements to total deceptions. Irritated by presumptions that north Wales was the centre of Welsh culture, he wrote documents showing that his beloved Glamorgan was the true beating heart. He claimed that his most accomplished forgery, Secrets of the Bards of the Island of Britain, was a copy of a manuscript, and composed high-quality poems he said were written by Dafydd ap Gwilym. People were misled because it was common in Iolo's day for scholars to copy old documents, because there was no university to police such work, and because he was persuasive. When he said a manuscript was ancient people believed him; and wanted to believe. Even in his own time he was legendary, the respected authority.

For many years Iolo was addicted to laudanum, an opium derivative, and no doubt it fired his fantasies. His wife Margaret begged him repeatedly to come home. One of his letters from London showed he did not know whether their three children were dead or alive. Usually a genial man, who in fun called himself 'leader of the fools of Britain', he could also be a venomous grudge-keeper. He died in 1826.

*154. Iolo by
William Owen
Pughe, 1805*

Years later, the bleak realization dawned that his labyrinth of invented tradition and literature had misled generations of scholars. To some he became an academic outcast. Yet much of what he wrote was reliable and brilliant. And he was not alone in his patriotic quest for an inspiring past: there were many such figures in Wales, England and Europe. Mining his huge archive in The National Library of Wales, scholars found a genius and an inspiring nation-builder.

THE CODE OF IOLO

Iolo Morganwg claimed that the bardic alphabet he invented had ancient origins. He devised a wooden frame with four-sided staves, each side bearing a line of poetry carved in his script. Iolo called it a peithynen. A number were made after his death, tributes from his disciples.

*155.
Poetry machine:
a bardic 'peithynen'
designed by Iolo
Morganwg*

NO SUCH PEOPLE

The story of the Welsh Indians was a myth that grew into a craze. In its time it had its uses in international politics. The tale said that in 1170 Madoc, a prince of Gwynedd, led an expedition across the Atlantic, landed in America and was the progenitor of a tribe of pale-skinned people known as the Madogwys, the Padoucas or simply the Welsh Indians.

156.
Tragedy in Hawaii: David Samwell's account of Captain Cook's death

In 1578 the Welsh mathematician and astronomer John Dee, an adviser to Queen Elizabeth, used the story to dispute the Spanish claim to America, saying that since Madoc had settled there three centuries before Columbus the British had title to the New World. The anti-Spanish Madoc story appeared once more when war flared between Britain and Spain in 1740, and again in 1790 during another dispute. Numerous and tantalizing reports of white Welsh-speaking Indians inspired a Madoc fever in America, Wales and London.

A
NARRATIVE
OF THE
DEATH
OF
CAPTAIN JAMES COOK.
TO WHICH ARE ADDED SOME
PARTICULARS,
CONCERNING HIS
LIFE AND CHARACTER.
AND
OBSERVATIONS
RESPECTING THE
INTRODUCTION
OF THE
VENEREAL DISEASE
INTO THE
SANDWICH ISLANDS.

BY DAVID SAMWELL,
SURGEON OF THE DISCOVERY.

LONDON:
PRINTED FOR G. G. J. AND J. ROBINSON, PATER-NOSTER-ROW.
MDCCLXXXVI.

NARRATIVE OF THE

or common stake, gave him a blow on the back of the head, and then precipitately retreated. The stroke seemed to have stunned Captain Cook: he staggered a few paces, then fell on his hand and one knee, and dropped his musket. As he was rising, and before he could recover his feet, another Indian stabbed him in the back of the neck with an iron dagger. He then fell into a bite of water about knee deep, where others crowded upon him, and endeavoured to keep him under: but struggling very strongly with them, he got his head up, and casting his look towards the pinnace, seemed to solicit assistance. Though the boat was not above five or six yards distant from him, yet from the crowded and confused state of the crew, it seems, it was not in their power to save him. The Indians got him under again, but in deeper water: he was, however, able to get his head up once more, and being almost spent in the struggle, he naturally turned to the rock, and was endeavouring to support himself by it, when a savage gave him a blow with a club, and he was seen alive no more. They hauled him up lifeless on the rocks, where they seemed to take a savage pleasure in using every barbarity to his dead body, snatching the daggers out of each other's hands, to have the horrid satisfaction of piercing the fallen victim of their barbarous rage.

count of many others, who were also eye-witnesses, I am confident, in saying, that he was first struck with a club. I was afterwards confirmed in this, by Kaireekea, the priest, who particularly mentioned the name of the man who gave him the blow, as well as that of the chief who afterwards struck him with the dagger. This is a point not worth disputing about: I mention it, as being solicitous to be accurate in this account, even in circumstances, of themselves, not very material.

I need

The idea of a lost Welsh tribe so enchanted Iolo Morganwg that he called for the sending of an investigative expedition. Saying he would go to America himself, he went into training, camping out and eating wild berries. His bardic friend David Samwell was also a Madoc-believer and wrote a poem, The Padouca Hunt, in support of the story.

Iolo never sailed, but John Evans of Waunfawr, Caernarfon, did. He was obsessed by the legend. In 1793, at the age of twenty-two, he crossed to America and started his long journey to find the descendants of Madoc. He was told that they were the Mandan tribe living in what is now North Dakota, 1,800 miles from Saint Louis. He took a gift, a Welsh Bible, that he intended to read to the Indians.

His two-year journey was an epic of adventure and suffering. The Mandans were hospitable, but after wintering with them Evans concluded 'there is no such people as the Welsh Indians.' He died in Saint Louis aged twenty-eight.

The chart he drew during his trek reached the hands of President Thomas Jefferson who gave it as useful information to Meriwether Lewis and William Clark when they set out in 1804 on the greatest of American exploration journeys. They found a route to the Pacific, opening the West to settlement. On the way they stayed with the Mandans and two men in their party noted 'these savages have the strangest language but they are the honestest savages we have ever seen ... we take them to be the Welsh Indians.'

DOCTOR AT SEA

At twenty-five David Samwell, 1751–98, a Denbighshire doctor and bard, joined Captain Cook's third world voyage of 1776–79. He became surgeon aboard HMS Discovery, one of the two expedition ships, and like many of the young men who sailed with Cook he recalled a special camaraderie. 'It is an article of faith with every one of us,' he said, 'that there never was such a collection of fine lads.'

In February 1779 he saw Cook clubbed to death by islanders in Hawaii and wrote a dramatic description. Home from the sea, he was an enthusiastic member of London Welsh literary groups and joined Iolo Morganwg in creating the gorsedd of bards. He took the bardic name of Dafydd Ddu Feddyg, David the dark-haired doctor.

157.

*158. Fishguard
for ever: sickles beat
the French, 1797*

A WOUNDED CLOCK

Concealed by gathering darkness
a force of 700 French soldiers and
a similar number of freed prison
ruffians scrambled ashore near
Fishguard in February 1797.
This was 'the last invasion of
Britain', an incursion that quickly
spluttered, a military damp squib.
The invaders were guided by a
local horse thief and led by
William Tate, a hopeless seventy-
year-old American adventurer.

That they were in Wales at all
was a mistake. They had intended to
burn Bristol and march to Liverpool
to distract attention from a planned landing
in Ireland. Contrary winds drove them to
Pembrokeshire. The invaders looted farms
and were soon drunk. One of them shot
a grandfather clock. Local yeomanry and
fencibles, or home guard, marched to face
the enemy. The French apparently mistook
a crowd of Welsh women in red cloaks for
soldiers, and Jemima Nicholas, a formidable
cobbler, famously captured French soldiers
at the point of her pitchfork. The invaders
surrendered on Goodwick Sands and
were marched to jail. Meanwhile, many
frightened people had fled inland.

English fears that Welsh admirers of
the French Revolution might support the
invasion were misplaced. The authorities
conspired to frame two nonconformist farmers
on treason charges. The prosecution was
based on perjured statements and collapsed.

THE BEEF ARMADAS

159.
*Montgomery
drovers, c.1885*

Along the country roads of Wales numerous Drovers Arms are monuments to a remarkable way of life. Cattle drovers urging their herds to the English markets were for centuries at the heart of Welsh business. 'The Spanish fleet of Wales,' Conwy-born John Williams, archbishop of York, called them in the seventeenth century, noting that they earned 'what little gold and silver we have.' Drovers transported cash, tax payments, goods and mail. Their business was improved by the banks they founded, the Black Ox Bank in 1799 and the Black Sheep Bank in 1810. From London they brought news, ideas, fashions and songs.

Hundreds of cattle, policed by corgis and cowboys, walked twenty miles a day. The pace was a gentle two miles an hour, to keep the animals fat, and each beast was shod to prevent lameness which might cause it to lose weight. Pigs were driven, too, and wore little boots, while geese had their feet tarred for the long march.

The drovers themselves were weather-proofed by broad hats, smocks and brown paper leggings. They were often joined by London-bound travellers wanting company and security. Some drovers were rogues, but to earn their mandatory droving licence they had to show integrity. Railways gradually took over the cattle-moving business and old-style droving ended in the 1860s. What everyone remembered about droving was the noise, the cattle lowing and geese cackling, the drovers shouting and whistling. It was heard for miles.

160.
*Next page:
Cilgerran Fair,
Pembrokeshire,
c.1885*

161.
*Examples of
local banknotes
(inserts)*

162.
Not hanged for a sheep: reprieve granted to Evan Jenks, sentenced to death for stealing a sheep, 1787

SCRIBBLING AND SLUBBING

Wool was for centuries at the heart of Wales. Manufacture of woollen cloth was the most significant single industry in the countryside until the 1850s, with Montgomeryshire, Merioneth and Denbighshire the chief wool centres. In the eighteenth century spinning wheels turned in thousands of cottages and many farms had hand-looms. The local pandy, or fulling mill, washed and thickened the cloth. Although mechanization gradually advanced, weaving by hand remained important and hundreds of men and women were engaged in the wool-

163. A fast clip: last shearing at Capel Celyn, July 1961

164. Account of the first Welsh sheepdog trials near Bala in 1873

The First Bala Trials.

MR. JAMES THOMPSON'S "TWEED."

Winner of the first Sheep Dog Trials of outstanding importance held in this country, Bala, 9th October, 1873. To the late R. J. Lloyd Price, Esq., of Rhiwlas, Bala, primarily belonged the honour of instituting the Bala Trials, under notable patronage, in 1873. The Trials were continued annually until 1877, but in 1878 they were merged in, or superseded by, the Llangollen Trials, which have been held annually ever since, except during the War. For permission to republish the above photograph acknowledgment is due to the proprietors of *The Field*, in the issue of which for 18th October, 1873, an excellent account of the first Bala Trials appeared. Mr. James Thompson, winner of the Trials, was a Scotsman from Dumfriesshire, resident in Wales.

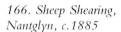

making processes of oiling, willowing, scribbling, carding, slubbing, spinning, winding, warping and sizing.

Newtown and Llanidloes prospered as manufacturers of flannel shirts and blankets and were notorious for their exploitation of weavers. Newtown boasted both an imposing Flannel Exchange and a flannel entrepreneur, Sir Pryce Pryce-Jones, whose customers included Queen Victoria and Florence Nightingale. He supplied flannel blankets to the Russian and Prussian armies. He also invented catalogue mail order and sent his first parcels from Newtown by stagecoach and later by special rail carriages to London. The bells of Newtown parish church rang in celebration in 1869 when the Queen placed a large order for flannel, and for that reason her portrait is incorporated in the church's main stained glass window. The wool business began to fade in mid-Wales during the 1860s but prospered in the Teifi valley of west Wales from the 1880s to the 1920s. Owners here maintained the tradition of low pay and exploitation of children who worked in the mills after school.

*165.
Spring Mills,
Llanidloes,
c.1880*

*166. Sheep Shearing,
Nantglyn, c.1885*

*167. Queen Victoria's
flannel: Broad Street,
Newtown, c.1900*

168.
Defying Rebecca: a Cardiganshire weir owner, a governor of the Bank of England, warned of retaliation against Rebecca wreckers, 1843

The Rebecca riots erupted in 1839. Men smashed turnpike tollgates in Carmarthenshire, foreshadowing a campaign of nocturnal gate-wrecking three years later. Across south-west Wales activists destroyed gates, burnt the hay ricks of magistrates and ransacked workhouses. Disguised in women's clothing they roamed the lanes as 'Rebecca's daughters', from the verse in Genesis saying that Rebecca's seed would possess her enemies' gates. A tollgate keeper was killed, the authorities summoned soldiers and London police to restore order and several rioters were jailed or transported to Australia.

The troubles arose from a stew of resentments. Population increase put pressure on the land. Harvests were bad. Farmers resented the burdens of tithes, high rents, and bullying justices. The tollgates that symbolized deprivation and oppression made easy targets. The network of gates around Swansea and Carmarthen forced farmers to pay heavily for bad roads. Tolls on lime, the chief fertilizer, were especially loathed. The Times sent a reporter, Thomas Campbell Foster, to cover the disturbances and his reports showed that the people had a just cause. A government enquiry led to turnpike reforms.

169. We're still here: years after the riots, Rebecca threatened to rise again against the tyranny of church tithes, 1854. Inset: 'Rebecca and her daughters assembled to destroy a turnpike gate', Ray Shuttleworth

ONE OF US

The fierce and bloody Merthyr rising of 1831 is lodged forever in the Welsh memory, a dramatic episode in the struggle for political reform. Merthyr was a seething and radical working-class stronghold whose people were infuriated by falling wages, rising debt and the ruthless confiscation of their property. Crowds demanding electoral reform rioted and freed prisoners. Another pay-cut and sackings in the ironworks stoked the fires of fury.

Early in June crowds gathered at Hirwaun, six miles to the west of Merthyr, and for the first time in Britain raised a red flag. Tradition says it was a cloth dipped in a calf's blood. The angry people swarmed into Merthyr, broke into shops, sacked the court house, recovered confiscated goods and put magistrates and constables to flight. The justices called for troops and eighty men of the Argyll and Sutherland Highlanders marched in from Brecon. An ugly row between magistrates, bosses and around 10,000 people degenerated into hand-to-hand fighting between soldiers and rioters urged on by the people's leader, Lewis Lewis. Troops in the Castle Inn shot dead around twenty-five demonstrators. The rebellion spread and raged throughout the district. Four days after the trouble started soldiers raised their muskets and stopped a crowd of more than 12,000 at Dowlais. Merthyr was at last brought under control.

In Cardiff, in July, a court sentenced two of the demonstrators to death. Lewis Lewis was reprieved and transported to Australia for life. Richard Lewis, aged twenty-three, also known as Dic Penderyn, was convicted of wounding a soldier and was hanged in Saint Mary Street, Cardiff. He was widely seen as the first working-class martyr in Wales, almost certainly innocent. Indeed, forty years later, another man confessed to the crime. Dic Penderyn was simply one of an angry crowd, and no doubt many who had been in it reflected: 'It could easily have been me.'

170.

THE CAMBRIAN.

SWANSEA, FRIDAY, AUG 12.

CONVICTED RIOTERS AT MERTHYR.

On Viscount Melbourne's granting the respite to the 13th inst. for *Richard Lewis*, as stated in our last, he promised to send the case which Mr. Price submitted to him, and which the Lord Chancellor admitted to be such as to render a respite proper, to Mr. Justice Bosanquet, for his report. Mr. Price, in the mean time, proceeded to Merthyr, and met the Judge at Brecon, from whom he learnt that a strong impression had been made, in confirmation of the evidence given in Court, of Richard Lewis's guilt, by a document appended to the petition of the inhabitants of Merthyr, admitting the guilt of the prisoners, *Lewis Lewis* and *Richard Lewis*, and of the justice of their sentence. This document was intended by the parties to have been submitted to the prisoners for their approval, *but it was never done.* Mr. Price, on the contrary, presented to the Judge a declaration, signed by the Chaplain of the goal at Cardiff, and others, that *Richard Lewis* had uniformly denied the charge of stabbing Donald Black. This declaration was forwarded through Lord James Stewart to the Home Office.—Mr. Price, after revisiting Merthyr, and collecting further evidence, waited finally on the Judge at Brecon, on Friday last, and laid before him a further statement, which we have had the privilege of perusing, and which we understand the Judge transmitted to the Home Secretary with his report. It exhibited to our view strong grounds for obtaining for the prisoner the extension of the Royal Mercy for a commutation of his sentence. Contrary to our hopes, however, the execution of *Richard Lewis* is to take place on the 13th (to-morrow), the day to which he was respited, the Home Secretary, Lord Melbourne, having given attentive consideration to the circumstances brought under his notice by Mr. Price since the trial, and having decided that he " *sees no grounds for mitigating the sentence.''* We cannot too deeply lament the issue of Mr. Price's benevolent and unparalleled exertions to save the life of a fellow-being; but we trust this case will prove the strong necessity that exists *for an early and complete revision of our Criminal Code.*

CARMARTHEN

PEOPLE MOVER

171. *London to Holyhead direct: Robert Stephenson's Britannia railway bridge across the Menai Strait opened in 1850. George Hawkins*

172. *Tan-y-bwlch station on the Ffestiniog line, c.1900*

By the 1840s the great engineer Isambard Kingdom Brunel was up to his cigar in railway schemes. His line from Merthyr to Cardiff, the first major railway in Wales, opened in 1841. In the same year his Great Western service started. Huge gangs of labourers drove tracks across the land in the orgy of railway speculation. 'The whole world is railway mad,' groaned Brunel in 1844. 'I wish it were at an end.'

Railways changed everything. Timetables made Britain into a single time zone. Stationmasters became new

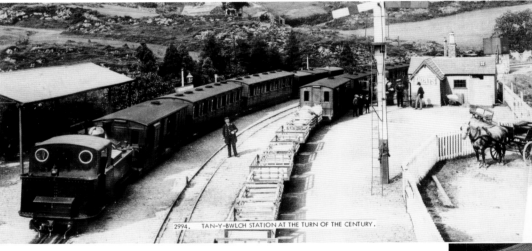

2994. TAN-Y-BWLCH STATION AT THE TURN OF THE CENTURY.

173. *Platform party: Machynlleth station, c.1885*

figures of authority. Lines reached
Holyhead in 1849, Pembrokeshire in
1856 and Aberystwyth in 1864. They put
an end both to the stagecoaches and the long-
distance cattle drives to England. They also
reduced the prices farmers paid to transport
meat, milk and fertilizer and made the
countryside more prosperous. A web of
tracks served the quarries of north Wales
and the southern coalfield.

Railways created the resorts of Llandudno
and Colwyn Bay, opened up spas like
Llandrindod Wells, made many villages
less remote and facilitated the movement
of eisteddfod-goers and choirs. They made
the countryside more accessible. In 1845
Thomas Cook organized his first commercial
Cook's tour, escorting 350 people on a
rail outing that included Caernarfon and
Snowdon. The crowds of tourists were
themselves a spectacle and local people came
to gaze at them. Fourteen hundred miles of
track were built in Wales in the thirty years
from 1840, all in private schemes. But there
was no planned network for the benefit and
unity of Wales as a whole.

*174. Steaming
through Welshpool,
1950*

A SELF-MADE MAN

The two identical statues of David Davies, at the docks he built in Barry and beside the road at his home in Llandinam, Montgomeryshire, depict not a dreamer but a hard-headed man with feet firmly planted. His business energy changed Wales and his own philanthropy, and the good works of his grandchildren, made a lasting impact.

Born in 1818, the eldest of ten children, he worked in a sawpit at eleven and went on to make his first fortune as a road and railway builder. He made another as a coal pioneer in the Rhondda. For anxious months he and his men tried to reach the steam coal seam that lay at a great depth and finally struck it, 660 feet down, in 1864. The Parc

*175.
David Davies
goes digging in
the Rhondda:
mining leases,
1860s*

and Maendy pits formed the nucleus of Davies's Ocean Coal company. In the 1880s he built the port of Barry to ship out his coal, avoiding the monopolistic charges levied by the Butes at Cardiff.

He was a plain man, thrifty, devout and self-educated, his gruffness leavened by his humour, proud to be known by the name he earned in his first job, Top Sawyer. The long speeches he made as a Liberal MP led Disraeli, the prime minister, to note that 'David Davies is a self-made man who worships his creator.' But he was on hand when it counted, providing the cash that enabled the university college at Aberystwyth to open in 1872. He also paid for chapels and hospitals. He died in 1890 and his son died only eight years later.

Thus the family fortune, generated by Rhondda coal, land and railways, devolved to the Top Sawyer's grandchildren, David, Gwendoline and Margaret. David, the first Lord Davies of Llandinam, became a Liberal MP and a generous philanthropist. He worked closely with Lloyd George and helped to raise a Welsh army in the first world war. He was president of the National Library, 1927–44. He and his sisters gave much money to fight and treat tuberculosis, funding many hospitals. David led and financed his own tireless campaign for world peace and built the Temple of Peace in Cardiff as the Welsh centre for the League of Nations.

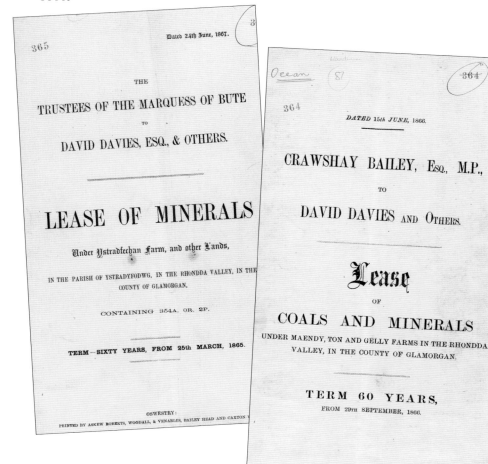

176. Digging for sunlight: Cambrian Colliery, Clydach Vale, Rhondda, 1914

All three remained loyal to their grandfather's principles and grew up with a strong sense of obligation to the mining communities which made their wealth. The girls, strictly raised, were carefully guarded. They never married and directed their talents to good works and the arts. They gave their great collections of French impressionists, gathered over fifty years, to the National Museum. Between the world wars they created at Gregynog, in the Montgomeryshire hills, a haven for craftsmanship, music, song and artistry, beauty for its own sake. Leading musicians took part in its festivals. In 1923 the sisters founded the Gregynog Press to create masterpieces of printing, illustration and binding. It faded, was revived in 1974, and still makes beautiful books. Always generous to the National Library, the sisters funded the completion of its art gallery in the 1950s, donated manuscripts including the De Grey Book of Hours and etchings by Rembrandt, Whistler and Augustus John.

177. David Davies, Llandinam

THE WIND CALLED THE TUNE

Seafaring runs like a stout cable through the story of Wales. Welsh and Welsh accents were part of the waterfront buzz across the world. Arriving in Valparaiso, Chile, in 1906, the crew of a Welsh barque found a dozen ships with Welsh captains. Alan Villiers, the Australian writer who sailed in square-rigged ships, said: 'Take the Lloyds, Llewellyns, Lewises, Hugheses, Davieses, Williamses and Jenkinses – or only the Joneses – from the British merchant service, and more than half of it would stop.'

178. Compass rose: Sarah Jane Rees, 1839–1916, was born in Llangrannog and taught navigation to seafarers in Wales, Liverpool and London. She was also a preacher, editor, feminist and temperance champion. As a poet she took the name of Cranogwen, c.1875

Before the age of railways and decent roads ships were the chief transport along the coasts of Wales, delivering food, timber, fertilizer, furniture and chapel organs. Shipbuilders cut timber from local woods and built on the beaches, relying on experience and an eye for a seakindly line rather than formal plans. These vessels were financed by local money, with merchants, farmers and chapel ministers buying the traditional one-sixty-fourth share. They were manned by local men, too, so that hopes and anxiety put to sea as well as investment. Most crews included a boy or two, for sea skills were learnt from an early age, and many Welsh youths chose the sea rather than life on a hill farm.

The schooners built at Porthmadog and Caernarfon and their sister ports loaded slate and made remarkable long-distance voyages. South Wales colliers delivered coal to the world. Sailing ships battled Cape Horn to

179. All hands on deck: old salts, Aberdyfi, c.1885

180. Lighthouse on South Stack, Holyhead,
William Daniell, 1813

181. Barmouth, William Daniell, 1813

182.
New Quay
in the 1880s

carry copper to Swansea. Liverpool, which
first flourished on the profits of the African
slave trade, became an Atlantic gateway,
the counterpart of New York. In the 1820s
the city's merchants built Britain's first
commercial telegraph. Ten semaphore stations
along the north Wales coast relayed messages
from Holyhead to Liverpool in five minutes,
telling shipowners their cargoes were on their
way. Welsh seamen were prized in Liverpool
for their knowledge and ability.
The Blue Funnel line hired
so many of them that it was
known as the Welsh Navy.

183. Schooners
and other vessels
in Porthmadog,
c.1880

*184. Sea guides:
Pilot boats heading
out of Swansea,
George Chambers,
1836*

COPPEROPOLIS

Swansea was first a Viking foothold, then a citadel of Norman conquerors, a target of Owain Glyn Dŵr's fury, a trading port of the Severn Sea, a fashionable saltwater spa, a porcelain maker, coal shipper and, at its industrial peak, the smelter of more than threequarters of the world's copper. Along the banks of the Tawe insatiable furnaces fuelled by abundant coal consumed shiploads of ore from Cuba, southern Africa, Australia and South America. By the 1820s a league of copper barons, Morrises, Vivians and Grenfells, were putting down dynastic roots. They drew on a pool of skilled coppermen. Swansea's long experience of metal-making led to the tinplate manufacture which prospered from the 1850s.

For years the masts of copper barques forested the harbour. The offices and workshops of shipowners, agents, chandlers and sailmakers filled the waterside streets. In the years when ships sailed regularly to Chile for copper ore Swansea seafarers knew Cape Horn as well as they knew the Mumbles. Finding dozens of Welsh ships anchored in Valparaiso an American captain growled: 'It looks as if Swansea owns the whole darned Pacific.' The voyages to Chile cost many vessels and lives. The last copper cargo brought to Swansea by way of Cape Horn arrived in 1905.

The shipowning Bath family of Swansea gave their vessels the names of letters in the Greek alphabet. One was the 700-ton barque Zeta. A baby girl was named after the ship and her actress granddaughter adopted it. The name of Catherine Zeta-Jones has an echo of Swansea's age of sail.

SPEAKING OF PRUNES

The first photographers were seen as magicians who could trap light in a box and snare the passing second. They were both makers and recorders of Victorian scientific progress. It was known in the 1820s that light darkened salts of silver. Louis Daguerre captured images on copper plate coated with silver iodide and his daguerreotype made its sensational debut in Paris in 1839. In March 1841 the Reverend Calvert Richard Jones made a daguerreotype of Margam Castle, the earliest-known photograph in Wales.

Since the daguerreotype produced no negative, each picture was a one-off. William Henry Fox Talbot improved on Daguerre with his Talbotype which produced a paper negative. He published the first book of photographs, The Pencil of Nature, in 1844; and the National Library has a partial copy. He spent much of his youth at Penrice in Gower and revealed the mysteries of the

185. Silver screen: the Margam Castle daguerreotype

camera to his cousins who themselves became photographic trailblazers in Wales. In those early years exposures were long and portrait sitters had to remain rigid. For the sake of a pleasing picture women were advised to frame their lips to the word 'prunes.'

Photography spread quickly in the 1850s and 1860s and most towns had their studios. Small calling card pictures of family and public figures were popular and applauded as 'the democracy of portraiture.'

John Thomas, from Cardiganshire, became one of the great shuttersmiths of Wales. He started as a travelling photographer in 1863 and charged sixpence for a portrait. His pictures of more than 400 preachers answered a public demand for portraits of pulpit celebrities. For forty years, until his

186. Jones bach, poet, c.1885

187. The tailor, Bryn-du, c.1875

188. Old lady, c.1885

189. Woman knitting, c.1875

190. 'Siân Phillip y Mynydd', c.1870

191. Sunday best: residents of Cerrigydrudion almshouses, Denbighshire

192. Diamond formation: one of John Thomas's popular compilations of Victorian pulpit personalities, c.1875

death in 1905, he travelled up and down Wales photographing people and landscapes, and later supplied pictures for O.M. Edwards's magazine Cymru. Three thousand of his negatives are in the National Library's collection of more than 750,000 images, by far the greatest archive of Welsh photographs.

Like John Thomas, Geoff Charles, a photojournalist for forty years, contributed significantly to photography and the Welsh memory. He retired in 1975 and gave his 120,000 negatives to the National Library. His many memorable photographs include his iconic portrait of the poet Carneddog leaving his farm, a horseback postman and scenes in the Tryweryn valley, haunting pictures of a vanishing way of life. Ron Davies and Raymond Daniel, too, are part of that tradition of Welsh photojournalism.

193. Tavern friend, Beaumaris, c.1875

194. Morris 'Baboon', c.1885

195. Two girls with cups, c.1875

196. Bo peep: Mary Dillwyn, 1816–90, a pioneer photographer in Swansea in the 1840s, had a notably informal style. She titled this picture 'Sally and Mrs Reed - Mary Lindsay peeping'

197. Bathing machines on Tenby beach, 1893

198.
*Pony express:
postman David
Lewis Jones,
photographed
in the 1950s,
delivered mail
to farms along
the road from
Tregaron to
Abergwesyn*

WHISTLER'S DAUGHTER

The cantankerous Merthyr ironmaster Robert Crawshay found solace in the new science of photography. He made his daughter Rose dress in various costumes and pose for him as a gypsy, a Swiss maiden and a peasant girl, summoning her to his camera by blowing a whistle. She also processed the pictures, tormented by the chemicals which inflamed and cracked her hands. Her father tried to keep her at home but at twenty-nine she defiantly married. Like a cruel character in a Victorian melodrama, he disinherited her. He died in 1879 and lies in a churchyard near Merthyr under a slab bearing the words God Forgive Me.

199. Poor Rose: she fled her father's tyranny and his photography

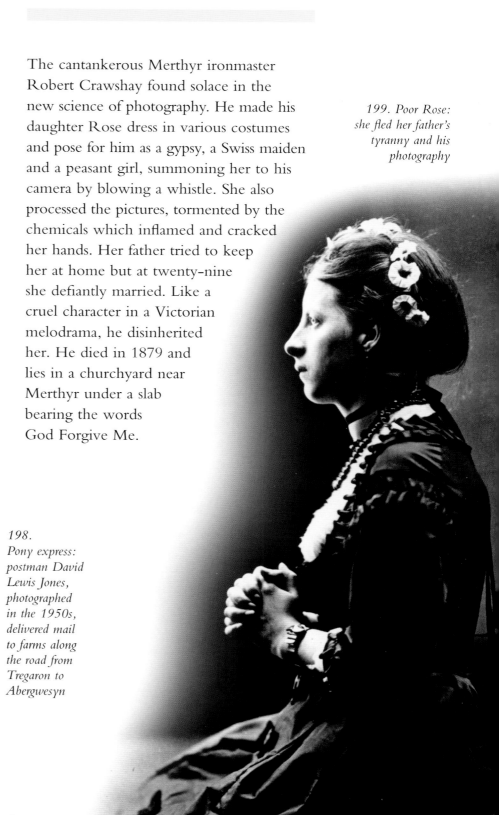

THE SINGING RIVER

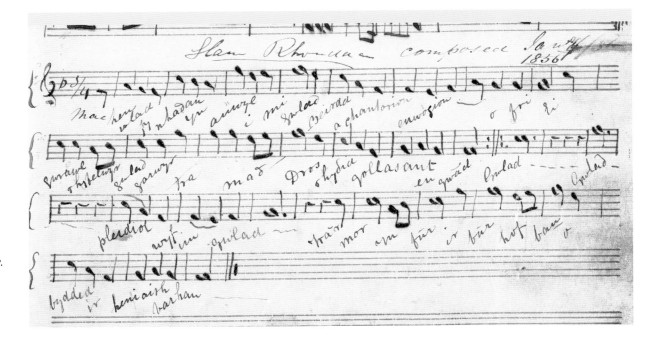

200. Annwyl i mi: the manuscript of Evan James's song of love for his country. The first recording, made by Madge Breese in 1899, is also in the library

201. Words: Evan James, c.1870

202. Music: James James, c.1890

Hen Wlad fy Nhadau, the national anthem of Wales, is stirring, singable and short, expressing a simple love of home and the hope that Wales and the Welsh language will live for ever. Evan James, a forty-seven-year-old weaver, a well-read man, fashioned the words as he walked beside the river Rhondda at Pontypridd in 1856. He gave them to his son James, aged twenty-three, who picked out a melody on his harp. They called their song Glan Rhondda and it was first performed by Elizabeth John in Capel Tabor at Maesteg in that year. It later became known by the words in its opening line, Hen Wlad fy Nhadau, Land of my Fathers, and grew in the Welsh consciousness. It became the national anthem by general assent. It was recorded on a wax cylinder by Madge Breese in 1899, the first record in Welsh, which is in the National Library. It was first sung by a rugby crowd at the match at Cardiff in 1905 in which Wales beat New Zealand.

The song came out of the blue. No one asked Evan and James James to compose it. It was not written by a leading poet and musician. Its authors wrote nothing else of significance. Possibly it was prompted by a letter Evan received from his brother who was doing well in America and urged Evan to join him. It was a time when many Welsh people were emigrating. Perhaps Evan's song was a letter to himself, a personal manifesto setting out what Wales meant to him: the land of his fathers he had no wish to leave. His son, a tavern musician with an ear for a lively tune, wrote the song as a jig. It so captured the national imagination that in the voices of the people it grew in majesty. The generations shaped it into the eloquent and haunting song of Wales.

OFF TO PATAGONIA IN THE MORNING

During his years at a Welsh chapel in Cincinnati Michael D. Jones of Llanuwchllyn in Merioneth observed that Welsh migrants rapidly embraced American life and lost their language. To people anxious to flee poverty and the oppressions of church and landlord in Wales, he offered a new dream, a Welsh colony at the earth's ends, safe from English influence. About 160 people responded to his vision and in May 1865 they gathered at Liverpool to join the ship Mimosa, bound for Patagonia, 7,000 miles distant. The vessel's strikingly-female figurehead had been replaced by a scroll. Michael D. Jones, who helped to fund the voyage, waved the migrants farewell.

Promised a paradise, these innocents landed in a harsh wilderness, dangerously unprepared and ill-clad. Many of them were from the coal valleys and only two had farming experience. In any case they arrived in July, the depth of the southern hemisphere winter, too late for planting. Men who made the forty-mile trek to the valley earmarked for settlement suffered such thirst that they drank their urine. The colonists were saved partly by native people who taught them to hunt and survive, by their own discovery of the uses of irrigation, and by money given by the Argentine government to buy supplies.

Slowly they built their colony, Y Wladfa, with chapels and schools and a senate elected by men and women over eighteen. Welsh was the first language in administration and commerce for thirty years and is still spoken, though superseded by Spanish. The Welsh colony was eventually absorbed into Argentina. The last large group of Welsh migrants, 113 people, sailed in 1911. Llwyd ap Iwan, Michael D. Jones's son, migrated in 1886 and was shot dead in 1909 by American outlaws, reputedly members of the Butch Cassidy and Sundance Kid gang. The Welsh colony was a small epic in the pursuit of dreams.

*203.
'A strong and self-reliant nation will grow in a Welsh homeland'–Michael D. Jones, c.1880*

Ysgol Cwm Hyfryd.

Ysgol y Rhyl

No. 4

CAMBRIAN EMIGRATION OFFICE, 41, UNION STREET, LIVERPOOL.

PASSENGERS' CONTRACT TICKET.

1. A Contract Ticket in this Form must be given to every Passenger engaging a Passage from the United Kingdom to any Place out of Europe, and not being within the Mediterranean Sea.
2. The Victualling Scale for the Voyage must be printed in the Body of the Ticket.
3. All the Blanks must be correctly filled in, and the Ticket must be legibly signed with the Christian Names and Surname and Address in full of the Party issuing the same.
4. The Day of the Month on which the Passengers are to embark must be inserted in words and not in figures.
5. When once issued, this Ticket must not be withdrawn from the Passenger, nor any alteration, addition or erasure made in it.

Ship _Mimosa_ of _450_ tons register, to take in Passengers at Liverpool, for _New Bay_ on the _Fifteenth_ day of _May_ 1865

NAMES.	AGES.	EQUAL TO STATUTE ADULTS.
Abraham Matthias	32	
Gwen do	23	
Mary A do		Inf.
Mary John	24	
John Thomas	18	
		4

I engage that the Persons named in the margin hereof shall be provided with a Steerage Passage to, and shall be landed at the Port of _New Bay_ in South America, in the Ship _Mimosa_ with not less than 10 cubic feet for luggage for each statute adult, and shall be victualled during the voyage and the time of detention at any place before its termination, according to the subjoined scale for the sum of £____ including Government Dues before Embarkation, and Head Money, if any, at the Place of Landing, and every other charge, except freight for excess of luggage beyond the quantity above specified, and I hereby acknowledge to have received the sum of £____ in ____ payment.

The following quantities at least, of Water and Provisions (to be issued daily) will be supplied by the Master of the Ship as required by Law; viz.—to each Statute Adult, 3 quarts water daily, exclusive of what is necessary for cooking the articles required by the Passengers Act; to be issued in a cooked state, and a weekly allowance of provisions, according to the following scale:—3½lb. Bread or Biscuit, not inferior in quality to Navy Biscuit, 1lb. Wheaten Flour, 1½lb. Oatmeal, 1¼lb. Rice, 1½lb. Peas, 2lb. Potatoes, 1¼lb. Beef, 1lb. Pork, 2oz. Tea, 1lb. Sugar, ½oz. Mustard, ¼oz. black or white ground Pepper, 2oz. Salt, 1 gill Vinegar.
N.B.—Mess Utensils and Bedding to be provided by the Passengers.

Signature in full _James Lamb_

On behalf of JAMES LAMB, of Liverpool.

LIVERPOOL, ____ day of _May_ 1865

Deposit £ ____ to be paid at the Office, 41, Union-st., Liverpool, one day before the above date for sailing, or deposit forfeited.

Balance £ ____

Total £ ____

NOTICE TO PASSENGERS.

1. If Passengers, through no default of their own, are not received on board on the day named in their Contract Tickets, or fail to obtain a Passage in the Ship, they should apply to the Government Emigration Officer at the Port, who will assist them in obtaining redress under the Passengers Act.
2. Passengers should carefully keep this part of their Contract Ticket till after the end of the voyage.
N.B.—This Contract Ticket is exempt from Stamp Duty.

Fernández

in Trelew (Y Wladfa)

Cabrero   Mrs Llewelyn Wms   Trelew

LLAWLYFR
Y
WLADYCHFA GYMREIG
YN CYNWYS SYLWADAU AR YR
ANGENRHEIDRWYDD A'R POSIBLRWYDD
O'I SEFYDLU,
HANES PATAGONIA, YN EGLURO EI HA-
DDASRWYDD I'R SEFYDLIAD,
Y DRAFODAETH A BUENOS AYRES AM
DROSGLWYDDIAD Y TIR,
BRAS-GYNLLUN O DREFN YR YMFUDIAD,
YN NGAYDA
DARLUNLEN O PATAGONIA.

Gan HUGH HUGHES,
YSGRIFENYDD CYFFREDINOL.

LLYNLLEIFIAD:
ARGRAFFWYD GAN L. JONES & CO., 44, HANOVER STREET.
1862

208. Fashion plates: Lady Llanover's suggestions for the well-dressed Welsh woman

LADY BUSY-BEE

Augusta Hall, Lady Llanover, born in 1802, was a wealthy and passionate supporter of Welsh music, literature and dance, a formidable woman who lived up to her imperious forename. Although a hesitant speaker of Welsh herself she ensured that her home at Llanover Court, near Abergavenny, rang with Welsh voices and music. She staffed it with Welsh-speaking servants, employed a harpist and insisted that the estate village chapel had a minister who was both bearded and Welsh-speaking. She took the bardic name of Gwenynen Gwent, the Bee of Gwent, and adapting the dress of country women, she created the 'traditional' Welsh costume of shawl and tall hat worn today by girls on Saint David's Day and other occasions. Her creation paralleled the popularising of the kilt and Highland dress in Victorian Scotland. She embraced the ideals of Iolo Morganwg and supported Iolo's son Taliesin.

After Taliesin's death in 1847 Iolo's manuscripts came into her hands and were deposited in the National Library in 1916.

A vigorous opponent of drink, Lady Llanover turned the public houses in the village into teashops. A local doggerel noted:

Grand house but small cheer,
Large cellar but no beer,
Lord Llanover lives here.

Lord Llanover was Benjamin Hall MP, a commissioner for works, whose name was given to the Big Ben hour-bell at Westminster. He strongly supported the right of people to have religious services in Welsh. Lady Llanover died in 1896 aged ninety-three and was escorted to her grave by twenty young women wearing 'traditional' costume.

THE FATHER
OF MYFANWY

209. Music for Wales:
Joseph Parry, c.1875

The prolific and innovative Joseph Parry was the founder of modern Welsh music. He regarded himself as an educator, creating music for the people. His love song Myfanwy is still sung frequently, more than a century after he wrote it. Apart from his hundreds of songs, anthems and hymns he composed an array of overtures, oratorios, cantatas, piano sonatas and a symphony. The first of his ten operas, Blodwen, was a popular landmark and had 500 performances.

Parry's life was a romantic journey. Born in Merthyr in 1841 he was a colliery boy at ten and in an ironworks at twelve. He grew up with the sound of the town bands. He moved with his family to Pennsylvania and worked in a steel mill. Following his successes at eisteddfodau in Wales in the 1860s a public fund was raised in recognition of his ability and it paid for his study at the Royal Academy of Music. In 1874 he was the first professor of music at the university college in Aberystwyth, taught at Swansea and Cardiff and was an eisteddfod adjudicator. His musical reputation is controversial. Some thought him sentimental and derivative. He was often impulsive and a showman. But much of his music was pioneering. It was melodious and accessible and the public liked it. People saw him as a national figure; as, indeed, he saw himself.

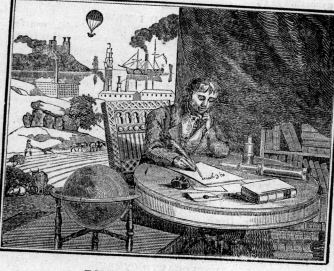

210. *Y Tories, going to the devil: James Cope's political cartoon, c.1834*

211. *Y Cymro, first issue, 1830*

212. *Y Celt, 1878, edited first by Samuel Roberts, Llanbryn-mair, prickly campaigner for individual rights and enemy of landlordism*

213. *Scourge: Thomas Gee, 1815-98, helped shaped a radical political outlook in Victorian Wales*

WHAT THE PAPERS SAY

The progressive liberal movement that found expression in Chartism and other agitation for political reform in the 1830s and 1840s led in the 1850s to the unshackling of the British press from government oppression. A tax on newspapers made them expensive and confined them to the governing caste. No member of the middle and working class could afford a daily paper. Abolition of the tax in 1855 and an appetite for news of the Crimean war opened the era of freedom and growth for the press. A huge readership was created in the Victorian expansion of industry, population, politics and literacy. The market demanded journalism and newspapers became the eyes and ears of the people. The idea grew that good government demanded a good press.

Like their counterparts in England the early newspapers in Wales were constrained by the government tax on news and knowledge and hostility to any commercial press. The papers were a by-product of the spread of printing presses. The first, The Cambrian, a weekly founded in 1804, reported the rising fortunes of its birthplace, Swansea. The North Wales Gazette followed in Bangor in 1808 and the Carmarthen Journal in 1810. The first Welsh-language weekly, Seren Gomer, started in 1814, failed after a year for lack of advertising but was relaunched as a monthly. The Monmouthshire Merlin, The Welshman, the Merthyr Guardian and the Carnarvon and Denbigh Herald began publishing in the 1820s and 1830s. To fill

their pages Welsh newspapers relied heavily on mining London papers for their news of foreign and religious affairs, shipwreck and murder.

Following the abolition of the newspaper tax Yr Herald Cymraeg was founded and the radical journalist Thomas Gee, of Denbigh, developed his family firm Gwasg Gee into a leading producer of books, magazines and newspapers, a catalytic force in Welsh politics and education. His weekly Baner ac Amserau Cymru, popularly known as Y Faner, founded in 1859, was the influential Liberal voice with a readership of 50,000 in the 1880s. Around forty Welsh-language papers flourished from 1880, supporting a new class of Welsh-speaking journalists.

The Western Mail, the first daily in Wales, was launched in 1869 to support the Conservative and Bute interests, and was funded by the Bute estate. It prospered with the aid of new printing technology, professional journalism and a wide variety of syndicated news and features. The demand for news of the first world war built a strong habit of reading the morning papers. Newspaper empires grew after 1918. The coal owner Lord Rhondda controlled a chain that included the Western Mail, Y Faner, Y Tyst, the Cambrian

*214.
Addysgydd,
the Educator, in
1823, the first
Welsh children's
paper, published
and illustrated
by Hugh Hughes*

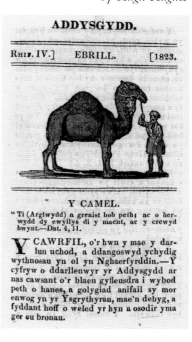

The Old Man of the Sea.

DAME WALES : Indeed, now, Mr. Asquith was very nice and sympathetic ; but I see I must give him no rest, if I am to get this load off my back.

[The imposition of the Coal Tax was deeply resented by the Welsh people, and continued appeals and protests were made to the Chancellor of the Exchequer in favour of its rescission.]

215.

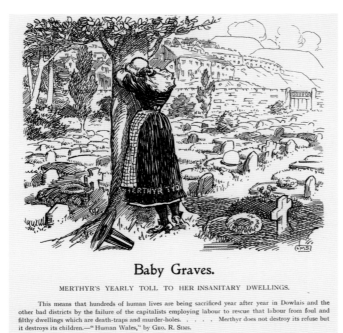

Baby Graves.

MERTHYR'S YEARLY TOLL TO HER INSANITARY DWELLINGS.

This means that hundreds of human lives are being sacrificed year after year in Dowlais and the other bad districts by the failure of the capitalists employing labour to rescue that labour from foul and filthy dwellings which are death-traps and murder-holes. . . . . Merthyr does not destroy its refuse but it destroys its children.—" Human Wales," by GEO. R. SIMS.

216.

A Path of Love.

[On July 20th and 21st, 1904, the King and Queen opened the King's Dock at Swansea, and the Birmingham Waterworks at Rhayader, amid scenes of great national rejoicing.]

217.

News, the Merthyr Express and Pontypridd Observer. The Berry brothers of Merthyr prospered as newspaper magnates: as Baron Buckland Henry was the first Welsh press lord, William became Lord Camrose and Gomer Viscount Kemsley. Until it was divided in 1937 the Berry Group owned four British national papers and forty-nine outside London. From the 1920s the number of newspapers in Wales, Welsh and English, declined. But some socialist newspapers thrived, perhaps as a counterweight to the Western Mail's unsympathetic view of the working class.

There was still a busy local press in Wales in the 1950s, but, increasingly, the newspapers entering most Welsh homes were London nationals. Falling circulations created problems. The creation of the Welsh Assembly inevitably posed challenges to reporters and editors. In the new circumstances there was a deficiency of information and opinion and no true national journalism, no genuine plurality of expression. Television and radio provide an excellent response to the demands for news and debate, but cannot entirely fill the gap that requires ideas and information on the printed page.

A Welsh eye: Joseph Staniforth's sharp cartoon commentaries reflected life in Wales for thirty years from 1889. Although he drew for the conservative Western Mail he attacked bosses and revealed the plight of the poor. His sturdy Dame Wales expressed Welsh opinion.

The Old Man of the Sea: Dame Wales berates the Chancellor of the Exchequer

Baby Graves: a comment on the numerous infant deaths at Merthyr caused by bad sanitation

A Path of Love: Wales greets King Edward and Queen Alexandra at the opening of the Swansea Dock in 1904

KILVERT COUNTRY

People still follow the paths trodden by Francis Kilvert who wrote engagingly about the people and countryside of Clyro in Radnorshire where he was curate from 1865 to 1872. He found wonder in small things and ordinary people and left a delightful if sometimes sentimental picture of Victorian rural life. Sensitive and unworldly, he wrote wistfully of the girls he met and kissed. Twice his hopes of marriage were crushed by parents who saw a penniless curate as a hopeless prospect.

He eventually married in 1879, aged thirty-nine, but died of appendicitis within five weeks. His widow burnt a number of his journals which referred to her. A selection from twenty-two remaining notebooks was published as Kilvert's Diary in 1938–40. Perhaps because of the erotic strain in the notebooks his niece destroyed nineteen of the twenty-two. Of the three that survive two are in the National Library.

218. Life in the country: Kilvert kept his diary from 1870 until 1879

DISTANT VIEW OF LLANTRISSANT AND THE CREMATION

DR PRICE'S HOME, LLANTRISSANT.

THE CREMATION OF DR PRICE, JANY 31st 1893.

HIS CHILDREN IESU GRIST AND PENELOPEN.

INTERIOR OF HOUSE

DR PRICE,

ARCH DRUID.

GWEN LLEWELLYN.

THE FUNERAL AT EARLY MORN.

IN MEMORIAM, 1893.

219.

THE PHENOMENAL DOCTOR PRICE

On his eighty-first birthday, in a druidic rite at Pontypridd, Doctor William Price pledged himself to Gwenllian, a girl of twenty-one. She became the mother of their baby Iesu Grist, Jesus Christ. When the boy died in 1884, aged five months, Doctor Price tried to cremate the body. People leaving a chapel thought they were seeing a human sacrifice. Doctor Price fled their fury and was rescued by police. Tried at Cardiff Assizes, accused of burning a body, he defended himself eloquently. The judge ruled that no crime had been committed, and the triumphant doctor was hailed as the pioneer of cremation in Britain. He was always a challenging man.

He was born in 1800 and his long life spanned the nineteenth-century story of the south Wales valleys. He saw them transformed into industrial and social crucibles. An active Chartist in the 1830s he fled to France disguised as a woman. All his life he was a waspish critic of clergymen and the coalowners and ironmasters he detested as 'bloodsuckers', but he was a friend of the unusual Francis Crawshay, whose essential humanity he admired. Price was a skilled doctor, a militant anti-smoker, fastidiously clean, a naturist, advocate of free love, Welsh patriot and a druid in the Iolo Morganwg tradition. He often wore a green uniform and a fox-skin hat with the legs and tail dangling down, his beard flowing. He also wore a scarlet one-piece garment like an outsize baby suit.

Doctor Price was eighty-four when he and Gwenllian had another son, and eighty-six when they had a daughter. At the age of ninety-two he called for a glass of champagne, drank it and died. Gwenllian sold tickets for his cremation at Llantrisant and 20,000 people witnessed it. The eccentric, passionate and legendary defender of his country and culture was consumed on the coal and wood pyre he designed himself.

220. William Price told his patients: 'Do as I say and you will get well. If you don't you will die.' He was a familiar figure in the Pontypridd district, often seen in his colourful costume

DOCTOR LIVINGSTONE, HE PRESUMED

Henry Morton Stanley was a poor boy from Wales who, courageous, daring and ruthless, made himself one of the greatest of African explorers. His baptismal record notes that he was born John Rowlands in Denbigh in 1841, the illegitimate son of a farmworker of the same name, and a bakery girl. A persistent local story suggests that his father was a Denbigh lawyer who avoided scandal by paying John Rowlands to admit paternity. The boy was educated at Saint Asaph workhouse and in his teens sailed to New Orleans where he was adopted by Henry Stanley, a wealthy businessman, who gave him his own name. Young Stanley joined the New York Herald as a reporter and, on assignment in 1871, began a search for the celebrated Scottish missionary-explorer David Livingstone, 'lost' for five years in east Africa. After an eight-month trek he met Livingstone in Ujiji, in modern Tanzania. The thirty-year-old Stanley had the scoop of his life, a story that astonished the world. He later crossed the heart of Africa, following the course of the Congo to the Atlantic, in 999 days. He also created the Congo colony for the king of the Belgians. He died in 1904.

221. Stanley of Africa: he gave Livingstone medicine, letters, newspapers and champagne

ELLIOTT & FRY

MISS VULCANA

One of the many intriguing photographs in the National Library collection shows the legendary strongwoman Kate Roberts, a star of the Victorian music hall in the early 1900s who took the stage name of Miss Vulcana. She specialized in hoisting men above her head on one hand. In another famous stunt, barely believable, she bent backwards until her hands rested on the ground and her abdomen supported a wooden platform on which two horses stood with their handlers. She urged women to care for their bodies and deplored the wearing of corsets. She met William Roberts, who ran a women's gymnasium at Abergavenny, and they lived together for fifty years and brought up six children.

222. Miss Vulcana: turn of the century pin-up, c.1895

A MAN OF
THE PEOPLE

Wales, said Owen Morgan Edwards, was 'a living thing, not a grave', and he spent much of his life demonstrating his country's vigour and romance in the popular journals he published. As an educator and prolific writer he influenced the development of modern Welsh culture. He was born in Llanuwchllyn, Merioneth, in 1858, and always retained an idealized view of the gwerin, the ordinary Welsh-speaking country people from whom he sprang. As young men, he, David Lloyd George and the budding politician Tom Ellis sat together and listened to Michael D. Jones, who had inspired the migration to Patagonia.

After a brilliant Oxford teaching career 'O.M.' edited his own successful monthly magazines Cymru and Cymru'r Plant which told highly-readable historical stories set in an unfailingly-delightful Welsh landscape. He became an MP, disliked the job and quit after a year. From 1907 he was the first chief inspector of schools in Wales, a post he held until his death in 1920, and in this work and his writing he continued to press the case for teaching children the neglected story of their own country.

224. Then ...

225. ... and later

223. O.M. Edwards:
builder of national consciousness, c.1910

THE PERSUADER

The best libraries in Wales in the mid-nineteenth century were kept in a few mansions at constant risk from fire, damp and vermin. Flames destroyed the treasures of Raglan, Hafod and Wynnstay, and it was the ever-present fear of fire that made the manuscript expert John Gwenogvryn Evans campaign for a secure National Library. Conflagration was only one of his nightmares. He knew, to his horror, of an Aberystwyth professor who used priceless books as a table for his tea and bread and butter.

Evans's association with Sir John Williams in the 1890s was a crucial element of the National Library story. Sir John, born in 1840 near Gwynfe, Carmarthenshire, was

*226. Peniarth,
in Pennant's
'A Tour in Wales'*

*227. Pyrophobe:
J.Gwenogvryn Evans,
George Phoenix, 1923*

a Harley Street obstetrician and, from 1886, a physician to the royal family. As a casual visitor to a book auction in Swansea in 1870 he heard someone murmur: 'This is the time to buy Welsh books, in fifty years it will be too late.' He resolved there and then to acquire the best possible collection and over forty years amassed 25,000 volumes. In 1896, with the dogged Evans as his go-between, he bought the important collection of manuscripts held at Shirburn Castle, Hereford. This included the only known complete copy of John Price's Yny lhyvyr hwnn and a ballad, a diatribe against tobacco, printed in Wales in 1718 by the pioneering Isaac Carter. Gwenogvryn Evans also piloted Sir John through the long and exasperating negotiation for the purchase in 1904 of the Peniarth library. Sir John paid £5,250 for the collection.

From the 1870s a patriotic impetus inspired the dream of a National Library. Through the 1890s the big question was where it should be built. A bitter contest developed between Cardiff and Aberystwyth. The government's decision, in 1905, turned on the sheer size and magnificence of the collections gathered by Sir John and by John Humphreys Davies, who would become the principal of the university college at Aberystwyth. Gwenogvryn Evans had persuaded both of them to pledge their books to the National Library, on condition that the library was planted in Aberystwyth. The government awarded

the National Museum to Cardiff. Sir John was the library's first president and before his death in 1926 he saw his dream take shape on the hill above the town, a Welsh Parthenon in granite and Portland stone.

*228.
The nation's
library:
Sir John Williams,
1840–1926.
Christopher
Williams*

THE RED SHIRT

Rugby football kicked off in Wales at Saint David's college in Lampeter and very quickly, in the 1870s, was embraced with passion in the towns and villages of the mining valleys. The crowds grew in a few years from hundreds to thousands. Much more than a mere game, rugby was woven into the community and industrial fabric, an expression of a national identity, a social cement. It was manly and dramatic, and, in a region where one man in three worked underground, it was also a celebration of the blessed open air.

*229. Accelerator:
Gareth Edwards*

*230. Old battlefield:
Cardiff Arms Park,
January 1959*

231. The other football: legendary John Charles won the first of thirty-eight Welsh caps at eighteen. Born 1931, he joined Swansea at fifteen, moved to Leeds, then Juventus, and towered as a great footballer, goalscorer and gentleman, never cautioned or sent off. He died in 2004

The managerial classes saw in rugby a means of channelling the energies of a simmering proletariat. Sometimes these energies boiled over and rival spectators transferred the battle on the field to the neighbouring streets. The valleys, after all, were a fast-growing frontier society. Several clubs in the raw early years were suspended because of the riotous behaviour of their crowds. Cardiff Arms Park was closed for five weeks after spectators manhandled the referee. Some local clergymen could only say 'We told you so.'

Chapel opponents of the game saw it as an enemy, as they saw the pubs where many teams met and changed for a match. Some hoped that the religious revival of 1904–05 would sweep it away. But nothing uttered in the pulpit could stop rugby's rush. As well as the prospering big clubs in Cardiff, Newport, Swansea and Llanelli there were numerous smaller fry playing for villages and industrial works: Moonlight Rovers, Dowlais Harlequins, Troedyrhiw Searchlights, Rhymney Pig's Bladder Barbarians, the forbidding Diamond Skull Crackers of Carmarthen, and the same town's threatening Shin Slashers.

From these muddy, slightly bloody and unruly beginnings the Welsh game emerged and bred its heroes. Out of the Cardiff Stars, for example, came the great centre-threequarter Erith Gwyn Nicholls who played for Wales for ten years from 1896 and captained the side ten times. He and others, like Rhys Gabe, Teddy Morgan, Arthur Gould, Dickie Owen and Dickie Jones, laid the foundations of all the legends.

THE VISION MAN

For more than a year in 1904–5 Evan
Roberts, a twenty-six-year-old miner,
led the last of the religious revivals in Wales.
It started in New Quay, Ceredigion, and
flamed through the country. Newspapers
covered it as a sensational human interest
story, with Roberts the celebrity-evangelist
drawing crowds into his ecstatic fervour.
Much of the phenomenon was propelled
by young men and girls and the press
published vivid reports of their streaming
tears, cries of anguish and the way they
collapsed dramatically into their seats.
Some clergymen condemned such unruly
scenes. The revival was perhaps a response
to a growing uncertainty in mainstream
religion and a reaction to rapid social change.

*232.
Revival service
in a coal mine,
J. M. Staniforth,
c.1904*

In any case it subsided as quickly as it had
flared. Evan Roberts suffered a nervous
breakdown and retired from public gaze.
He died in Cardiff in 1951.

*234.
A newspaper
sensation*

*233. 'God seized hold of me.
He pressed me down to the earth.'
Evan Roberts, 1904*

SPLITTING THE QUEEN

From the end of the eighteenth century slate quarrying was the chief industry of north-west Wales. It gave birth to roads, harbours, railways, towns, a shipping trade and a vigorous human culture. At its peak in the late nineteenth century 18,000 men quarried 451,000 tons, more than nine-tenths of the British output. Gigantic terraces cut into mountainsides and vast piles of waste rock are a legacy of colossal endeavour.

Most of the slate was used for roofing. Throughout the Victorian age Welsh slate schooners delivered regularly to Germany, France, Scandinavia, America and elsewhere. Ten narrow-gauge railways carried slate out of the quarries and into Porthmadog, Caernarfon, Y Felinheli and other ports. They replaced the carts and packhorses of the early years. Quarried rock was skilfully split into slates of standard sizes called queens, princesses, duchesses, countesses and ladies.

235.
Blue remembered
quarries: Dinorwig,
1999

Most quarry entrepreneurs were major Gwynedd landowners like Richard Pennant, later Lord Penrhyn, and Sir Watkin Williams Wynn. Pennant ploughed his family's Jamaican sugar plantation money into slate. Quarrymen formed themselves into teams of four or six who struck their own pay deals with managers. Known as the bargain this arrangement gave the men pride in being independent contractors rather than employees. Many workers lived in quarry barracks from Monday to Saturday and ate and entertained themselves with song, debate and poetry in a hut, a caban. Each caban elected a chairman, treasurer and a 'policeman' who punished swearing with a fine.

The work was, of course, dangerous. Conditions in villages were often bad and tuberculosis was rife. More than half the Welsh migrants from Wales into America in the 1840s were quarry people. The quarries contributed to the radical political tradition from which sprang men like David Lloyd George. During y streic fawr, the great quarrymen's strike of 1900–03, Lord Penrhyn sought to break the bargain system and prevent the men forming a union. Infantry, cavalry and police moved into Bangor and Bethesda to meet threats of trouble; and striking quarrymen sang a song about 'hordes of policemen speckling the land and defending betrayal.' Bitterness

236. *A roof over the world's head: quarrymen at work. Llechwedd Quarry, Blaenau Ffestiniog, c.1890*

between strikers and the cynffonwyr, the blacklegs who went to work, divided communities and percolated through the generations for much of the century.

237. *Slate awaiting shipment at Felinheli on the Menai Strait, c.1880*

LETTERS FROM THE WIZARD

238.
'A Nonconformist
genius' by Spy

239. Fine and dandy:
the rising star. Photo of
young Lloyd George,
1890

David Lloyd George and Winston Churchill towered as the great British statesmen and war leaders of the twentieth century. Lloyd George's social reforms showed the way to the future management of Britain. The National Library has thousands of the letters he wrote to his family. They throw revealing light on his thinking, ambition and controversial character.

He was born in Manchester in 1863 and raised in a comfortable home in Llanystumdwy by his widowed mother and his uncle Richard Lloyd, who ran a shoemaking business and was a Baptist preacher. At sixteen he started training as a lawyer in Porthmadog and he and his younger brother William founded the law firm that financed LG's political career. His radical mind was shaped by the dramatic social and political currents in Wales, the bitter divide between nonconformity and the established church and between landlords and tenants. Rural poverty, tithe wars and the growing national awareness in Wales influenced his ideas.

In 1890, aged twenty-eight, a rebellious man of action and flexible principle, he became Liberal MP for Caernarfon Boroughs, an ambitious outsider determined to challenge the English world. In his Welshness, passionate speaking and sensual charm, people saw a wizard and blue-eyed enchanter. He reached hearts and minds through newspapers and his speeches to crowds rather than through parliament and in his early thirties was the ascending star of Welsh politics.

His gossipy letters to his wife Margaret and brother William, in a mixture of Welsh and English, form an extraordinary running commentary to his career. He was president of the board of trade, 1905, chancellor of the exchequer, 1908, author of the 'people's budget' in 1909, and champion of the national insurance legislation of 1911. With this early framework of the welfare state he sought to kindle 'warmth and glow' in grey lives.

In the first world war he was munitions minister, secretary for war and, from 1916, the prime minister ruthlessly committed to victory. The pressures of war reduced his letter-writing output mostly to scant notes but in his speeches he was as eloquent and

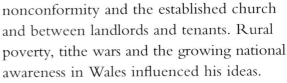

240. The burden
of power. Portrait
by Augustus John,
1920

241. Boy with wizard, c.1890

242. Lloyd George
in Punch, 1910

visionary as ever. He harnessed the power of the press. He believed strongly in the personal touch, the man-to-man deal, a trait that led some to regard him with suspicion, as a fixer. In this manner he negotiated the creation of the Irish Free State in 1921, a triumph soon poisoned by civil war.

He fell from power in 1922 and the Liberals were cast into disarray. In the 1930s he strongly admired President Roosevelt's New Deal economic measures. He was also, for a time, impressed by Hitler's policies which reduced unemployment. He failed at first to perceive the brutality of the Nazi regime. From 1936, however, the reality was all too plain.

Lloyd George died in 1945 and was buried beside the Dwyfor at Llanystumdwy, where he had played as a boy.

243.
In a vain search for peace, Lloyd George met Hitler in 1936, at Berchtesgaden

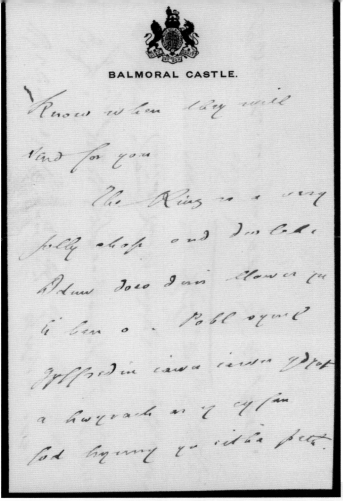

244.
Lloyd George writes home on court mourning paper after the death of Edward VII, 1910

MY ROUND LITTLE WIFE

Lloyd George and Margaret Owen married in 1888. In fifty years he wrote her more than 2,000 letters and notes, many of them candid, intimate and impassioned. He anguished over Margaret's refusal to leave Wales and join him in London. 'Drop that infernal Methodism,' he wrote, 'the curse of your better nature and reflect whether you have not rather neglected your husband. I have more than once gone without breakfast. I have scores of times come home in the dead of night to a cold dark and comfortless flat without a soul to greet me. You have been a good mother. You have not – and I say this now not in anger – not always been a good wife.'

When she did travel from Cricieth to join him he was delighted. 'Your placid, brave spirit has a soothing effect on my turbulent and emotional nature.' On another occasion he wrote: 'In spite of occasional sulks I cannot do without my round little wife.'

He wrote to her in English peppered with Welsh, sometimes to hide an indiscreet comment. His opinion of King George V in 1910 was: 'The King is a very jolly chap

245.
A scolding from a breakfastless man

ond diolch i Dduw does dim llawer yn ei ben' – 'but thank God there is not much in his head.'

Lloyd George began his long affair with Frances Stevenson in 1912. She became a figure of some power in his household. They lived in Surrey. Margaret never left Cricieth. He would never divorce her and he married Frances after Margaret's death in 1943. His children did not attend the wedding.

SEE YOU AT BRACCHI'S

From the 1890s cafes run by Italian immigrants were a familiar part of the streetscape and social life of south Wales. The owners worked a productive seam selling tea, hot Oxo and Bovril, sweets, cakes, cigarettes, ice cream and fizzy drinks flavoured with lemon or sarsaparilla root. Typically the cafes had glass shelves, mahogany counters, mirrored walls, large confectionery jars and marble soda fountains. Although the owners had a variety of names, Conti, Basini, Rabaiotti, Figoni, Carpanini, Sidoli and others, the cafes were popularly called Bracchis, after the pioneers who started in Newport, Aberdare and the Rhondda.

They traditionally opened early in the morning and closed at eleven at night. Many made sandwiches and cooked lunches and teas. They also sent out boys with handcarts to sell ice-cream in summer and chips in winter. They were favourite meeting places, especially in winter when they were warmed by large stoves. People lingered over tea and couples courted. The cafes were slightly exotic and had a touch of class. As 'temperance bars' they were an alternative to the pubs.

The cafe families were mostly from Bardi in northern Italy, part of the large Italian exodus to Europe and America caused by poverty on the land. Bardi men went first to London but were drawn to Wales by the coal boom, forging a link between their home town and Wales and making their unique contribution to valleys society.

*246.
Coffee Italian-style
at the Express Cafe:
Andrew Cavacuitti,
proprietor, greets a
regular customer, 1989*

Welsh Pit Disaster. The Intermittent procession of Coffins from the Pit.

Benton
138 George St
Glasgow. 19.

247. The black day:
stunned villagers at the
Universal colliery in
Senghennydd

THE FIERY PIT

248.
Local clergy
giving help

In 1913 Welsh coal owners reached the summit of their prosperity. The southern coalfield produced 46 million tons and all but one per cent of it was cut by hand. Shareholders earned dividends of twenty per cent or more. During this time inflation devalued miners' wages by twenty-five per cent. The dangers underground were well known. In 1901 eighty-two miners died in an explosion at the colliery in Senghennydd, near Caerphilly. In October 1913 an explosion 2,000 feet down in the same pit killed 439 men and boys, the worst disaster in Welsh mining history. A skilled photographer, William Benton, recorded the

aftermath in twenty-five pictures, a moving portrayal of the community's grief. Their immediacy transcends the years. They were sold as postcards. The mine owners were fined £10 for breaches of regulations.

The scene outside the mortuary at Senghenydd at the Universal Pit.

249. Carrying their comrades' coffins

THE SHOWMAN OF THE VALLEYS

Bestriding two eras of entertainment in Wales, William Haggar was one of the last of the travelling theatre showmen and one of the first cinema pioneers. Born in 1851 he ran away from home to be an itinerant actor in the portable wood and canvas theatres that moved from town to town staging robust comedies and melodramas. These were popular with the crowds, frowned on by chapels, but often approved by magistrates for keeping men out of the pubs. Haggar ran his own travelling theatre in Wales and from 1898 added screen shows to the entertainment.

He then launched himself as a film maker and in 1901 produced a fifteen-minute crime drama, The Maid of Cefn Ydfa, which was probably the first screen fiction in Britain. Over the next eight years he blossomed as the outstanding early film director in Wales and made around forty comedies and dramas. In 1909 he set up as a cinema proprietor in Aberdare. His Electric Palace was famous and his 700-seat Kosy Kinema,

opened in 1915, set the standard for luxury. The growth of cinema and the outbreak of war in 1914 put an end to the travelling theatres. In its collection of early films The National Screen and Sound Archive of Wales, housed in the National Library, has one of the few surviving Haggar films, A Desperate Poaching Affray, a four-minute drama made in 1903 showing a gunfight between police and poachers. Haggar died at Aberdare in 1925.

250. Cut to the chase: the innovative William Haggar pioneered the thrills of pursuit in his film A Desperate Poaching Affray, 1903, set in Pembrokeshire

CARROT VERSUS BEEF

The rough glamour of boxing had great appeal in Wales, especially in the mining valleys. Local heroes punched their way from poverty to celebrity. The years from 1900 to 1914 were a vintage time both in boxing and rugby. Jim Driscoll, from Cardiff, was bantamweight champion of Britain, Europe and the world. Jimmy Wilde, the 'Tylorstown Terror', world flyweight champion in 1916, lost only four of his 864 bouts. Frederick Hall Thomas, of Pontypridd, who took the ring name of Freddie Welsh, was to many minds the greatest of them all.

A detailed and fascinating record of his career is in the four scrapbooks found in the attic of his home in America and acquired by the National Library. Crammed with cuttings from British and American newspapers they form a blow by blow chronicle of a self-made man. Freddie Welsh had a shrewd understanding of what reporters liked and shaped his own image as a boxer with a difference, a bookworm champion who relaxed with Ibsen's plays, a vegetarian who trained on carrots.

251.

He was in his teens when he left Pontypridd to make his life in America. In Kansas in 1905, out of work and hungry, he took to boxing for a living and showed his talent, winning twenty-five fights and losing none. Two years later he came home to establish himself in the British ring and make his name in Wales. He quickly succeeded and became the darling of his home town, so much so that a crowd seeing him off at Pontypridd station serenaded him with the popular song Farewell My True Love.

He became British lightweight champion and in a sensational fight at Cardiff in 1910 he beat Jim Driscoll. In London in 1914 he became world lightweight champion. Back in America he was a wealthy celebrity and continued to cultivate his image as a boxer who lived on lettuce and literature. 'Vegetarian Philosopher Phenom' the Los Angeles Times called him.

But in the melodramatic way of so many boxing careers he began to drink and fray at the edges. He lost his world title in 1917 and fought his last fight in 1921. He and his wife parted and his fortune dwindled away in the economic depression. In 1927 the last headlines reported his suicide in a New York hotel room. He was forty-one, and one of the finest athletes made in Wales.

Winning a World's Championship on Carrots, Peas and Spring Water

"Vegetables Did It!" Declares Freddy Welsh, Who Has Wrested the Lightweight Title from Willie Ritchie—Whereupon Bob Edgren Flashes a Pen Picture of the Foxy Little Fighter That Has the Movies Beaten to a Standstill.

By Robert Edgren.

ALEXANDER THE GREAT swept through Asia Minor on a diet of goat's flesh and fermented wine carried in goat skins. Freddy Welsh became lightweight champion boxer of the world on carrots and peas and spring water. I leave it to the reader to decide which was the greater performance.

Of course Freddy's diet included a few other things, but neither goat's flesh nor any other kind of flesh. His usual draught of spring water was occasionally varied with a glass of milk or buttermilk, which was his nearest substitute for the "Dutch courage"

Freddy Welsh's characteristic grin when telling about the virtues of the non-meat diet. He admits that he does not force his pet Airedale to follow the dietary precepts of the master. "Oh, yes, I give the poor dog a bone," the champion is fond of saying with a smile.

When threshing season came along Freddy Welsh hired himself out as a thresher, and for several weeks worked hard in the fields. To his amazement he found that his endurance was greater than that of the other men; that he never f... .... hard fourteen-hour day's .....

"Vegetables," said Fr... taking his share from the ... eating corn, carrots, pea... tables of all kinds. He ha... last, and he stuck to his ... glances of the farmer's ... jeers of his co-workers. ... rule was in the matter ... boiled at each meal.

With his threshing fiel... to New York. He was s... way, not Freddy Welsh, v... again and registered at ... few dollars left, but vege... this village, they were so... vegetables, and New Yor... and peas and beans and ...

FRED WELSH AND JIM DRISCOLL.
[Photo. C. Corn, Cardiff.]

They set him to work mopping floors. And while he was mopping away one night he picked up a page torn from The World. It was a "Help Wanted" column, and Freddy saw an ad. calling for a "gymnasium instructor" for an uptown gymnasium run by a gentleman named Knipe.

Freddy dropped his mop, glanced at the clock, and rushed out. At the Knipe gymnasium he found a hundred men waiting in line, and the doors closed. And here he showed the first symptom of that remarkable foxiness that was to have so much to do, later on, with Freddy's annexing of the world's championship. Freddy glanced down at the overalls he wore and instantly formed his plan of battle. Pushing his way through the waiting crowd he announced loudly. "I'm the plumber; don't keep me waiting." Reaching the door he hammered on it with his fist and called: "Here's the plumber; open up!" An assistant opened the door cautiously to let Freddy come in, then locked it again.

"What d' you mean? We don't want no plumber," said the assistant.

"Huh!" said Freddy loudly. "What did the doctor telephone the boss for then? I want to see Dr. Knipe in a hurry. I've no time to waste. Get a move on you."

Attracted by the noise, Dr. Knipe came out. Freddy at once explained his strategem and Knipe thought he deserved a trial.

The duties of the "instructor" were to box with pupils. Freddy was told he'd have to fight his way through the list of other candidates already picked. He knocked the first out in two minutes, outboxed

...nns

...eddy, de-
...ressing room.
... Welsh when he
... from him as he
... all comers and
...mber Welsh both
...egetarian. He's

... meat eater when
...s his name was
...d left home at
... world. He had
... and buy a few
...ontreal, where he
...reddy, like other
... a nice evening's
...eal. He hadn't
... or so on a train.
...t, when he was
... some farmhouse.
...gry.

...k as a mechanic's
...l him the price of
...nt. Half rations
...rlust had him in
...d West as a regu-
lar hobo, riding on brakebeams and beating his way from town to town until he reached South Dakota. Between treks he worked as waiter in little restaurants, where he fattened up quickly on a hash diet. The hash was the main attraction for Freddy in those unregenerate and hungry days.

You see, the GREAT IDEA hadn't struck him yet. Here he had been passing through thousands of miles of vegetables, raw, of every kind. And he

still wanted the fleshpots.

But there came a time when Welsh was out of a job and every hashery had more help than it needed. Freddy took to camping out in the "jungles," as the hobo camps were called.

One day, starving as usual, he climbed a farmer's fence and stuffed himself with raw corn, which he gnawed hungrily from the cob. Lamb's Chinee, accidentally discovering the wonderful flavor of roast pig by licking his fingers after digging a defunct porker from the ruins of a burnt hut, had no greater feeling of ecstasy. Right on that spot Freddy Welsh became a vegetarian in practice.

Here was food with no hash house drawback. He experimented and found a number of vegetables which he could eat raw. For weeks Freddy dodged the hash houses and ruminated around among the vegetable gardens and corn patches. Any farmer was quite willing to let Freddy eat all the raw corn he wanted. Usually the farmers guffawed and looked on Freddy as a curiosity, for in South Dakota and the Middle Western States farmers have a saying that "corn is fit for hawgs." Only the most poverty stricken would think of putting boiled corn on his own table.

(Continued on page 17.)

255. *Y Gadair Ddu:
the chair at the poet's
home in Trawsfynydd*

256. *A popular postcard by J. Kelt Edwards
mourning the death of Hedd Wyn in 1917*

THE DARKENED
THRONE

Under the bardic name of Hedd Wyn, Ellis
Humphrey Evans, a Merioneth shepherd and
poet, wrote an awdl, an ode in strict metre,
for the National Eisteddfod chair competition
in 1917. He left for France in June with
his unit of the Royal Welch Fusiliers and
on July 31 was killed, aged thirty, at the
battle for Pilckem Ridge in Flanders. At the
eisteddfod in Birkenhead in September the
announcement that the chair had been won
by Hedd Wyn, and that he had been killed
in action, filled the audience with grief.
His winning poem was called Yr Arwr,
The Hero. The empty chair on the stage
was draped in black, a striking symbol of
loss. It was carried in poignant procession
to the Evans family farm near Trawsfynydd
where it remains in a
room kept as a shrine.
A film of his life,
directed by Paul
Turner in 1992,
was the first
Welsh language
film nominated
for an Oscar.

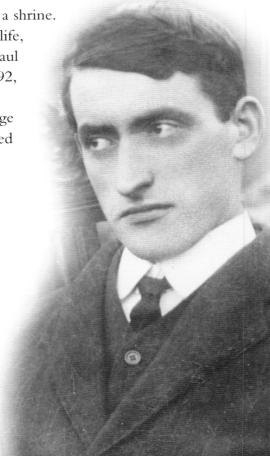

257. *The cross
from Hedd Wyn's
grave in Flanders,
brought home to
Wales, May 1952*

258.
*Hedd Wyn,
c.1914*

LETTER TO
A SOLDIER

The novelist and journalist Kate Roberts, born in 1891, was one of the best and best-loved of the twentieth-century writers in Welsh. She was first driven to write, as a form of catharsis, by the horrors of the first world war. The National Library has a loving letter she wrote to one of her brothers who was killed in the fighting; and one from him to her. Another brother's health was broken during the war. Much of her writing concerned lives lived in hardship. It was also shaped by her upbringing at Rhosgadfan, a totally Welsh-speaking Caernarfon quarrying community. She and her husband Morris

Williams published Y Faner newspaper and she ran it herself for ten years after his death and also wrote literary and political columns. She and Saunders Lewis corresponded for many years, commenting on each other's work, on literature and politics and life in Wales, and their letters are in the library. She died in 1985.

259. Kate Roberts

261. News from home and the farm. Kate Roberts's letter to her brother at the front.

260. 'Writing for children isn't my strong point' - letter from Kate Roberts to Saunders Lewis

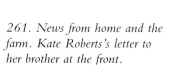

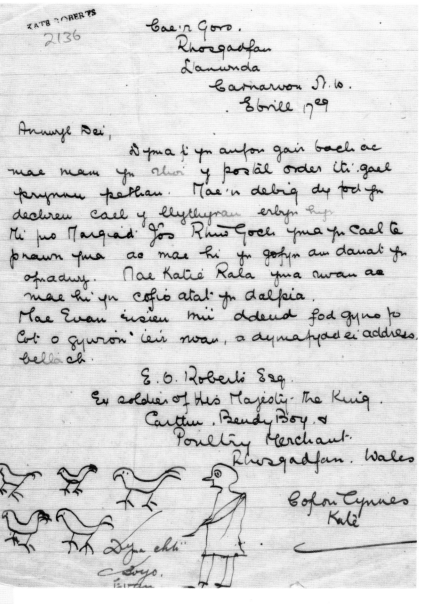

262. Stills, with
original tinting, from
The Life Story of
David Lloyd George:
Lloyd George played
by Norman Page;
addressing a crowd;
at home with his
daughter; people
emerge like ghosts
from a wall

THE FLOATING LORD

Lord Rhondda, the former David Alfred Thomas, was a coal tycoon who had a powerful influence on the growth of mining in Wales. He had a political career as a Liberal MP for Merthyr. In May 1915 he and his daughter Margaret were returning from a business trip in New York aboard the Cunard liner Lusitania. The ship was torpedoed off the south-west coast of Ireland and sank in twelve minutes. Margaret and her father became separated. Both were rescued.

Margaret clung to a plank and was hauled half-dead from the sea. Her father climbed into the last lifeboat as the ship rolled over. They were reunited at Queenstown. The lifejacket Lord Rhondda wore, signed D.A. Thomas, is in the National Library. During the last years of the war he served as the government's food controller.

263.

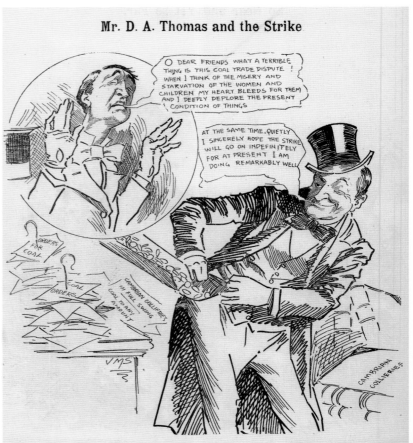

Mr. D. A. Thomas and the Strike

264. Filling his
pockets: Joseph
Staniforth's cartoon
shows D.A.Thomas
profiting from a
coal strike, 1898

THE RIDDLE OF THE FILM

The telephone call from Lord Tenby, Lloyd George's grandson, was intriguing. 'There's a pile of old film canisters in my barn. You might be interested in having a look at them.' The staff of Wales Film and Television Archive, what is now The National Screen and Sound Archive of Wales based in the National Library were certainly interested. One of them drove to Hampshire in a van, retrieved the canisters from the barn and brought them to Aberystwyth for examination. The films were cinema treasure: newsreels and interviews and, above all, the original negative of a feature film, The Life Story of David Lloyd George.

This was a complete surprise. Researchers identified the footage as the mysterious 'lost film,' the silent cinema biography of Lloyd George made in 1918 and confiscated in a bizarre fashion just before its premiere. A lawyer visited the producers, gave them £20,000 in cash and took the film away. They never saw it again.

The film was a vivid epic directed in a big, broad-brush style ahead of its time by Maurice Elvey, Britain's most prolific film creator. It was produced by Harry and Simon Rowson of the Ideal Film Company. Lloyd George had originally supported the film. It showed his progress from country boyhood to radical politician and war leader. The crowd scenes were remarkable. The film was a patriotic portrayal of a prime minister at the height of his fame. But a few days before its scheduled first showing in 1918 the Rowsons were told that Lloyd George himself opposed it.

Perhaps he feared public resentment of a popular film glorifying him. Perhaps the portrait of a war leader was less relevant in the aftermath of conflict. Possibly the film's robust crowd scenes were thought dangerous at a time when there was fear of workers' revolt. Perhaps politicians were in any case uneasy about the impact of the new medium of cinema. But, more significantly, Lloyd George's mistress Frances Stevenson did not like it. She saw hypocrisy in the depiction of Lloyd George's blissful family life with his wife Margaret and 'begged David not to let it be shown.'

Whatever the reason, the film was not screened and the negative lay for years in a barn. Lord Tenby himself had no idea what was in the canisters. The restorers spent twenty months repairing and editing 137 rolls, keeping the film true to Maurice Elvey's vision. Elvey himself once said it was the best film he ever made. In 1996, seventy-eight years after it was suppressed, his masterpiece had its premiere in Cardiff. Its drama still resonated.

GATHERING LILACS

Ivor Novello was born David Ivor Davies in
Cardiff in 1893, the only son of a sometime
rent-collector, known as Honest Dave, and
a formidable, flamboyant and ambitious Mam.
Clara Novello Davies, named after a diva her
father admired, styled herself Madame and
taught singing at Llwyn yr Eos, Nightingale
Grove, her home in Cowbridge Road.
Gowned, crowned and coruscatingly jewelled,
she toured America with her Royal Welsh
Ladies Choir. 'Mam,' recalled Ivor, 'always
thought on a big scale.'

In 1914, after leaving Magdalen College
choir school in Oxford, he wrote his ever-
appealing song Keep the Home Fires
Burning, the start of his long career as
a popular entertainer. During his time in
the Royal Naval Air Service he survived
two plane crashes. He wrote a dozen
plays, but his greatest successes were his
extravagant and romantic Ruritanian musicals
Glamorous Night, Careless Rapture, The
Dancing Years, Perchance to Dream and
King's Rhapsody; and such songs as We'll
Gather Lilacs and Someday My Heart Will
Awake. He starred in more than twenty
films, a matinee idol all his life, but his true
love was music and the theatre. His talent
was, perhaps, underrated in his native
country. He died a few hours after a
stage performance in 1951.

*265.
Ivor Novello,
c.1930*

*266. Mam:
the self-styled
Madame Clara
Novello Davies.
'No such word
as can't' was
her favourite
expression,
c.1894*

*267. Mam's
nightingales:
The Royal Welsh
Ladies Choir,
Chicago, 1893*

268. Wales and its youth:
Ifan ab Owen Edwards, photograph
from original painting by Alfred Janes

270. Llyfr Mawr y Plant was the first quality book
for Welsh-speaking children. It was first published
in 1931 and the chief characters in the stories, Wil
Cwac Cwac, the fox Sion Blewyn Coch and their
friends, entertained generations of children. The tales
were written by Jennie Thomas and John Owen
Williams, and illustrated by Peter Fraser

A PURPOSE IN PLAY

In 1922 Ifan ab Owen Edwards founded
Urdd Gobaith Cymru, the Welsh youth
movement, taking his inspiration from
the children's club started by his father
O.M. Edwards. The Urdd's ambitious project
was to encourage the interest of children and
young people in their country and culture
and, especially the Welsh language. From the
outset the Urdd emphasized outdoor activities,
expeditions, summer camps, sailing, canoeing,
walking, skiing; in a word, fun. It runs
residential centres with a strong 'outward
bound' flavour and for many thousands of
people the Urdd camp has been a memorable
part of summer. The movement's annual
eisteddfod is established as a cultural landmark.
Today the Urdd flourishes as one of the
major Welsh youth movements and has
more than 51,000 members.

THE FASTEST
MAN ON EARTH

THE MINISTRY
OF HAPPINESS

Five times between 1924 and 1927 Malcolm
Campbell and the Welsh driving ace J.G.
Parry Thomas broke the world land speed
record on the broad sweep of Pendine
Sands on the Carmarthen coast. Thomas,
an outstanding engineer who was once
chief designer at Leyland, broke the record
twice in 1926. Campbell beat his time early
in 1927, reaching 175 miles an hour. Parry
Thomas returned to Pendine in March that
year to challenge his rival again. His car
was a twenty-seven litre blue and white
giant called Babs. He was close to the
record speed when a driving chain burst
through its guard and struck his head, killing
him instantly. Grieving local people dug
a hole beside the beach and buried the
wrecked car there. It was recovered
in 1969 and restored.

271. Babs exhumed:
forty-two years after
Parry Thomas's car
was buried in Pendine's
dunes it was dug up
to be rebuilt, 1969

An hour of children's stories marked
the start of broadcasting in Wales on 13
February 1923 by the pioneering station
5WA in Cardiff. It set an avuncular tone.
An orchestra played Entry of the Gladiators
and a message from Lloyd George was read.
Music, news and a weather report followed.
The lord mayor welcomed the introduction
of high culture into the homes of the poor.
The Welsh language made its broadcasting
debut when Mostyn Thomas sang the folk
song Dafydd y Garreg Wen. The Western
Mail hailed the station as 'the Ministry
of Happiness.' Before long an engaging
informality developed and listeners were
greeted with the words 'Hullo Comradios.'

The studio in Castle Street, soundproofed
with blankets, was a hot and airless room
from which swooning musicians staggered
to gulp air. Thereafter broadcasting remained
in other senses a hot and prickly business,
a source of cultural anxiety and
political argument. The inevitable
difficulty in striking the balance
between two languages was as

272.

sensitive as it was enduring. But broadcasting assisted powerfully in the shaping of Wales's modern identity.

From the start the London-centred BBC adamantly refused to consider Wales. Broadcasters and public had perforce to be a pressure group struggling for recognition and money. The strength of Welsh loyalty and aspiration was for years a source of wonder at the BBC. In 1927 a committee inquiring into the Welsh language said that 'BBC policy is one of the most serious menaces to Welsh.' Rigid John Reith, the austere BBC head who detested Wales and the Welsh, complained that 'Welsh nationalists are impervious to reason.'

Nevertheless, a separate Welsh region of the BBC was founded in 1935 marking the start of broadcasting's fuller part in Welsh life with an output of drama, documentaries and the music of the new BBC Welsh orchestra. In 1937 the Welsh region was awarded its own wavelength. Mai Jones's long-running variety show Welsh Rarebit started in 1938. In 1940 it first broadcast the song 'We'll Keep a Welcome' which had a profoundly emotional effect among audiences whose fathers, brothers, sons and daughters were in uniform. The programme was popular throughout Britain, part of a post-war radio age that in retrospect had a golden glow.

273.
With Big Mike:
Iorwerth Thomas MP
and Gwynfor Evans,
1951

CLUB AFFAIRS

NEW PRESIDENT
BQMS DAVIES

SINCE his birth at Sebastopol, Monmouth—shire, October, 18, 1908, B.Q.M.S Davies' main hobby has been rugby. From his school team he graduated into the Panteg team, of which he was secretary from 1925 to 1933.

As a nonplayer he has refereed local school games and coached schoolboys. In this camp his work as chairman of the Rugby Committee has gained for him a Y.M.C.A award. His ambition is to be a Welsh Union senior referee.

In 1926 he joined the Territorials serving continuously in them until the outbreak of war, when he joined a training regiment in Exeter. Finally volunteering for the East he visited Egypt, Iraq, Palestine and Syria before going on the desert. July 1, 1942 and El Daba were the date and place of capture, and after three months in Derna and Caserto hospital he spent 3 weeks in P.G. 66 before finally settling down in P.G 70, & then IV B.

He is a married man with one daughter and earned his living as a steelworker in Panteg steel works.

Will any club member who is an instrumentalist with his own instrument please contact Emrys Evans, 49 B.

LOCAL BOY MAKES GOOD

OPPORTUNITY favours the few, and 15 year old Stanley Baker of Ferndale can thank the good fates that sent a London talent scout to the local Working Men's Hall, when he took part in a performance given there by his Secondary School Dramatic Society. That was in 1942.

As a result he was taken to London and trained in film work, eventually appearing in a film called "The Underworld" with John Clements and Mary Morris. After finishing this he returned to Ferndale and started work in an ammunition factory.

But again fortune was kind to Stanley. Emlyn Williams sent for him to take part in his new play & Stanley will thus act side by side with his famed countryman.

The Royal Visit

During their visit to South Wales on March 30 the King and Queen were accompanied by Princess Elizabeth. A tour of the Trading Estates was a feature of their trip.

Note

THE purpose of this supplement is mainly to deal with those items of sport and social activities that cannot be adequately dealt with in the hand magazine. Members who cannot attend general meetings will thus be kept in touch with club news.

New President appointed and Working Committee formed

AT the special meeting held on Monday, May 29, the Club administration was drastically reorganised. BQMS Davies was elected President after RSM Tooze had resigned for personal reasons. The latter subsequently accepted the newly established post of Vice-President.

An assistant secretary was appointed to help E. Evans, and for this post Trevor Hodges was elected. In addition three extra members were appointed to form, with the five other officials, a working committee to handle all club affairs.

Two Sub-Committees

This committee is composed as follows:— B.Q.M.S Davies (Pres.). R.S.M Tooze (V. Pres.), E. Evans (Sec.) Mark Grant (Treas.) Trevor Hodges (Ass. Sec.) George Evans, Harry Hopkins and Idwal Davies.

Since then it has been divided into halves, one consisting of the President, Vice President, Treasurer and Ass. Secretary, to handle club sports and the other composed of E. Evans, Id. Davies, Harry Hopkins and G. Evans to take care of the Social side of activities.

General Meeting

In future all General Meetings will be run on a social basis. Club business will be dealt with and finished at the beginning and the latter period will be devoted to things of an interest nature— lectures, sing-songs, etc. Anyone willing to give a talk, dance, or stand on his head please contact E. Evans 49B

Club Badges

At present 70 badges have been produced, but lack of material is holding up further supplies. The President has suggested that the badges already made be issued to huts on a percentage basis.

Members going out on Kommandos will be issued with a badge and if possible a gift of cigarettes.

Welsh Classes

Welsh classes commenced on Friday, June 9, at 6.30 pm in the Rec. Hut. Names for enrolment are to be given to Id. Davies or E. Evans, both 49 B.

Authority has been given to the Central Committee to deal with urgent matters without referring to the Club.

The Choir

ON Wednesday night, May 31, a number of the boys met together in the Rec. Hut for a Sing-Song, and before the evening was out, a Welsh choir had been born.

Subsequent singing practices have seen a steady increase in the number of voices, and great keenness is being shown by each of its 45 members.

The first function will be to sing at the Social Evening being held shortly. A lot of hard work is still required of its members so that the items may be rendered in a way worthy of Welsh voices.

When they are, it is hoped to see the choir takes its place in Camp Entertainment.

WELSH BEHIND THE WIRE

Men who endured captivity in prisoner of war camps knew the importance of keeping up their spirits and were famously ingenious in entertaining and feeding themselves, as well as planning escapes. Servicemen from Wales, held in Stalag IVB seventy miles south of Berlin in 1944-45, produced ten issues of their magazine Cymro, as neatly handwritten as a medieval manuscript and illustrated with watercolours and drawings. As with all POW publications there was only one copy, passed from man to man. The pages were filled with scraps of news from home, poetry, stories in Welsh and English and articles on rugby, sports heroes and Welsh regiments. A report in 1944 under the headline Local Boy Makes Good recorded that the young Stanley Baker of Ferndale won a film part after a talent scout saw him on stage at the Working Men's Hall.

The camp's Cymric Club published the state of its finances: cigarettes and chocolate were the currency. It was reported that the club's treasurer was 'in the clink' and that 'when possible members in the cooler get the equivalent of a bar of chocolate.'

The National Library also has news sheets from the Cymdeithas Gymreig founded at the Ruhleben internment camp, Berlin, during the first world war. Four thousand British men and boys, trapped in Germany by the sudden onset of war, were held there.

274. *Left: the prisoners' paper*

275. *News from home and elsewhere. The prison camp newspaper reports the death in action of the former Welsh rugby international Captain Maurice Turnbull in Normandy in 1944*

CAVE ART

When war loomed in 1939 the British Museum, the National Gallery and other London institutions evacuated thousands of paintings, books and assorted treasures to sanctuaries in Wales. By rail and road the first load of paintings left Trafalgar Square on August 23 and the last on September 2. Roads beneath low bridges were excavated to permit lorries with large pictures to pass through. Van Dyck's giant portrait of Charles I negotiated a bridge with threequarters of an inch to spare.

Most of the National Gallery's pictures were transported to a slate quarry cavern, 300 feet deep, near Blaenau Ffestiniog. Five thousand tons of rock were blasted to create more room. A staff of fourteen looked after the pictures. An underground storage chamber was also created in rock near the National Library. Many pictures and artefacts were kept in country houses and, wherever they were stored, the temperature, humidity and ventilation had to be maintained at steady levels to prevent damp and rot. At a mansion near Aberystwyth blankets were soaked in a nearby stream and hung in the picture rooms. In 1945 the treasures were taken from their Welsh caves and safe-houses and restored to London.

THE BOX IN THE CORNER

In 1953 a competition to find a Welsh word for television attracted a thousand suggestions. The winner was teledu. Television or teledu, the medium became a political and cultural cockpit. The battle in the 1920s–30s to secure a Welsh radio wavelength was repeated in television from the 1950s. London frowned at Cardiff's favouring of a form of broadcasting home rule. BBC Wales started in 1964 and debate intensified.

English and Welsh shared one channel, too narrow a bed for many. The arrival of independent television in the 1950s did not alleviate this particular problem. Depending on one's point of view there was either too much Welsh or too much English, a matter aggravated by extraordinary transmission difficulties in a mountainous country. Argument intensified because broadcasting was seen as crucial to the future of Welsh. Saunders Lewis's resonant radio broadcast on the fate of the language in 1962 persuaded many Welsh speakers that there was a crisis they had a duty to address. The broadcast spawned Cymdeithas yr Iaith Gymraeg, the Welsh Language Society which, from 1963, pressed for more Welsh in education, public life and administration. Demonstrators demanded bilingual roadsigns and official forms.

278.
Actor, singer, comic genius, Ryan Davies, pictured in 1965, was the backbone of television comedy in Welsh until his death at forty in 1977

279. *'Life for the Welsh language', 1971*

280. Rocketing raspberries! SuperTed was created in 1978 by Mike Young of Cardiff in bedtime stories he told his four-year-old son Richard. The adventurous teddy bear made his television debut in Welsh on S4C in 1982 and in English on the BBC a year later. Translated into many other languages the stories became popular with children throughout the world

From the early 1970s campaigners focused increasingly on television. The belief grew that only a Welsh-language channel would resolve the crisis. In 1977, BBC radio broadcasting was divided linguistically between Radio Wales and Radio Cymru. In 1979 the Conservative government construed the referendum rejection of a Welsh assembly as a loss of national resolve and broke its promise of a Welsh television channel. Gwynfor Evans, president of Plaid Cymru, vowed to starve himself to death and the government re-made its pledge. Sianel Pedwar Cymru, S4C, began broadcasting in 1982 under the leadership of Owen Edwards, son of Sir Ifan, grandson of O.M., a family continuity of commitment. Broadcasting in Wales, a key element in the broader movement for a national expression is a story of determined persistence.

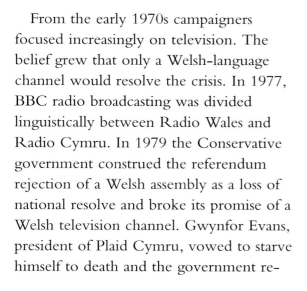

281.

NUTSHELL TRUTH

A sharp line and a few words, brevity and immediacy, truth in a nutshell: the cartoonist's art. Leslie Illingworth was one of the top practitioners of the twentieth century, a witty commentator on war and peace, statesmen, tyrants and ordinary people coping with life. He was born in Barry in 1902, worked for the Western Mail and joined the Daily Mail in 1939. He drew there for thirty years and he was also chief cartoonist at Punch. More than 4,500 of his cartoons are in the National Library.

282. Illingworth's view of Michael Foot as 'the white knight of the Left', complete with CND shield, after winning the Ebbw Vale by-election in 1960

283. ... and his view of himself

*284. In fading hope:
rescue workers in
the wreckage of
Pantglas school*

THE LOST CHILDREN

Swollen and destabilized by rainwater the mountain of colliery waste above the mining village of Aberfan roared down the slope just after nine o'clock on the morning of 21 October 1966. The black sludge and rubble swamped Pantglas primary school, killing 116 children and twenty-eight adults.

'We knew in these valleys,' a miner said, 'that sudden death was always a part of going to work; but not of going to school.'

The tribunal of inquiry sat for seventy-six days. The National Coal Board, headed by the defiant Lord Robens, denied all responsibility for the disaster. The people feared an official whitewash but there was none. The tribunal report in 1967 blamed the Coal Board, saying the disaster could and should have been prevented. It noted the Board's indifference to safety measures in respect of tip stability. The report told 'not of wickedness but of ignorance, ineptitude and failure in communications.'

In the aftermath of the disaster public grief and anger motivated a campaign to make safe or remove the black Fujis of colliery waste thrown up in more than a century of mining. The people found a voice. A positive legacy of Aberfan was the determination that replaced official and public apathy regarding the damaged landscape and dangerous waste. Restoration, tree planting, river-cleaning and the creation of parks on once-ruined land, a commitment to making amends, became a remarkable feature of the retreat from coal. The work continues.

Most of the people of Aberfan stayed in their village, close to each other and within sight of the hillside where their children and friends lie buried. Theirs remains a moving story of resilience and community.

WESTERN MAIL

THE NATIONAL NEWSPAPER OF WALES

SATURDAY, OCTOBER 22, 1966   4d.

for COMMERCIAL PHOTOGRAPHY
WESTERN MAIL & ECHO STUDIOS
CARDIFF 33022

SOUTH WALES EDITION

83 KILLED, 60 STILL LOST

The two-million-ton black avalanche which slid half-a-mile down from the coal tip above Aberfan and engulfed a farm, crushed Pantglas Junior School and swept away a row of cottages in Moy Road is clearly shown in this aerial picture by a Western Mail photographer. The main rescue operation is centred just behind and to the right of the remains of the school building in the centre of the picture. The houses in the path of the creeping slurry were evacuated during the late afternoon and other houses in the area showed cracks because of the pressure.

Wilson promises inquiry of the highest order

Duke of Edinburgh to visit Aberfan

THE Duke of Edinburgh is flying to Wales today to visit the disaster area, it was announced late last night. Lord Snowdon arrived in Cardiff early today and drove straight to the disaster scene.

■ Among the messages of sympathy received was one from the Queen, and another from the Prince of Wales.

■ Water board officials appealed to housewives not to hoard water. The slip smashed through trunk mains, but supplies were restored later by using supplementary mains.

■ More than 1,000 miners, 150 specially-picked Civil Defence officers and the NCB's entire rescue team rushed to the area. Thousands of volunteers, hundreds of lorries and earth-moving equipment and 15 doctors stood by. Almost 100 soldiers from South Wales regiments were ready to move in if needed.

■ Miss Jane Morgan, a 21-year-old teacher from the adjoining secondary school, said she watched helplessly as boys drowned. "After they were dead you could hear them screaming," she said. "Then as they opened their mouths torrents of water from the burst water-mains seeped through and drowned them."

■ Two years ago a former Mayor of Merthyr, the late Mrs. Gwyneth Williams, warned of the danger from the tip. "We have a lot of trouble from slurry, causing flooding," she said. "If the tip moves, it could threaten the whole school."

Disaster fund set up

EARLY this morning the bodies of 75 children and eight adults had been found under the massive avalanche of colliery waste which engulfed a school, farmhouse and row of houses at Aberfan in the Merthyr Vale yesterday. Between 50 and 60 were still missing.

A medical spokesman at the demolished Pantglas School said, "We are still checking on these provisional figures."

Thirty-six children were taken to hospital during the day.

As rescuers toiled through the night under the blaze of arc lights several collapsed. Eighteen were taken to hospital and eight detained.

Men digging into the 40ft. deep mound of debris last night found the bodies of the deputy head teacher, Mr. D. Bernon, and five children.

A rescuer said, "He was clutching five little children in his arms as if he had been protecting them. He and five children died clutching each other."

WESTERN MAIL REPORTERS

area last night the Prime Minister, Mr. Harold Wilson, promised an inquiry at the highest level into the tragedy. An NCB spokesman said a preliminary investigation showed that recent abnormal rainfall had caused the tip to move.

Mr. John Beale, Merthyr's Director of Education, said last night, "We can now say that approximately three classes, totalling 66 in number, came out safe in totality."

He said that it had been established at seven o'clock that out of the 190 children on the roll at the adjoining secondary school, 194 were known to be safe.

"The picture is still in the

on the Prime Minister's visit to police headquarters at Merthyr, said that Mr. Wilson had been given a full report from each of the emergency services involved, and had expressed his satisfaction at the manner in which things had been carried out.

Sympathy

Mr. Wilson has appointed Mr. Cledwyn Hughes, Secretary of State for Wales, to take charge of all operations.

The chief constable said the tip was, at the moment, under control, and water had been diverted.

the Queen and from all parts of the world poured into South Wales.

Parents were still filing into the town's small Welsh chapel at eight o'clock last night to identify the bodies of their children, but only a few of the 36 lying on the pews had been identified.

Mothers were advised not to enter the temporary mortuary, and only fathers were allowed to view the bodies.

Tragedy struck at about 9.15 a.m. yesterday just after the children at Pantglas School began their morning lessons—the last before they broke-up for a half-term holiday.

Luckiest schoolchildren were those of between five and seven who, because they start school later in the morning, missed the disaster. Some others were saved because a bus bringing them to school was late, and 29 others were rescued and rushed to hospital at Merthyr Tydfil

A WANDERING
MUSHROOM

The National Eisteddfod is an institution unique and necessary: annual general meeting, reunion, paseo, Gangetic dip, corroboree, waterhole, celebration of poetry, song, the Welsh language and Welsh people themselves. The essence of all eisteddfodau, national, district or village, is the competition which sharpens performance and gives children the confidence to face an audience.

The word derives from eistedd, to sit, and means a session. Its ancestor was the bardic gathering of medieval times. A famous eisteddfod was held at Cardigan in 1176. Bards were a class of historians, genealogists, tutors and storytellers but, above all, poets who had mastered the intricate and strict rules of composition in Welsh. Poetry was the only expression of the nation's artistry and a source of delight. A prince was always pleased to be hailed a poet.

286. National winner: Rhydwen Williams crowned and acclaimed at Swansea 1964, and saluted by the archdruid and the herald bard, whose sword of peace is never bared

287. Far right: Watched by a crowd at Aberystwyth, the gorsedd in traditional procession at the National Eisteddfod, 1952

Today, as it was long ago, poetry is pre-eminent at the Eisteddfod and large crowds watch the presentation of the two top prizes. The crown is awarded for a pryddest, verse in free metres, and the chair for an awdl, verse in the traditional strict metres. Like certain singers and rugby players in Wales champion poets are counted as popular princes.

The bardic way of life declined in Tudor times as the patronage of the gentry withered. Iolo Morganwg revived what he claimed was an ancient bardic and druidic tradition, staging the first ceremony of his Gorsedd Beirdd Ynys Prydain, or circle of British bards, in London. This became an inseparable part of the Eisteddfod from 1858 and flourished as a pageant, with its archdruid,

trumpets, a sword of peace and a horn of plenty, and robes of white, blue and green. In the 1860s The Times called the Eisteddfod 'a mischievous and selfish piece of sentimentalism, a foolish interference with the natural progress of civilization and prosperity.' Some still think so today, but the poets and the pageantry prevail.

Eisteddfod-goers are drawn not only to the craftsmanship of poets, but also to a great social gathering, a summer party. The festival has no fixed abode. It roams the country, siting itself in the north one year and in the south the next, erupting in the landscape each August like a gigantic and beneficent mushroom, ready to nourish its faithful pilgrims.

288.
Cynan in a convertible, 1964: a commanding and genial presence in the administration and pageantry of the National Eisteddfod, Sir Albert Evans-Jones, second from the left, was known universally by his bardic name of Cynan. Thrice winner of the crown, winner of the chair, archdruid, president of the eisteddfod court, and enjoyer, he was the complete, rounded eisteddfodwr. He shares the car with gorsedd figures Brynallt, left, and William Morris, right

LIVES IN PICTURES

Ivor Novello led the way as the first Welsh film star. The bright stream of talented actors who followed in the 1950s and 1960s included Richard Burton, Stanley Baker, Hugh Griffith, Kenneth Griffith, Siân Phillips, Meredith Edwards, Donald Houston and Rachel Roberts.

Richard Burton, born Richard Jenkins at Pontrhydyfen, the twelfth of a miner's thirteen children, was gifted with a thrilling voice and a leonine presence. His power resonates in films like Look Back in Anger, Becket, The Spy Who Came in from the Cold and Who's Afraid of Virginia Woolf? He enjoyed notoriety as well as fame, loved being a drinking raconteur, twice married Cleopatra, in the form of Elizabeth Taylor, and revelled in his Welshness. His Rhondda-born friend Stanley Baker, a master of menace

289.
Stanley Baker,
c.1958

290. Roman cricket:
Richard Burton plays an
innings during a break in
the filming of Cleopatra

291.
Richard the Voice in
Jack Howell's film
Dylan Thomas,
1962

and taciturnity, starred in The Cruel Sea, Violent Playground, The Guns of Navarone and Zulu. Hugh Griffith won an Oscar for his role in Ben Hur. He also appeared in A Run for Your Money, Lucky Jim, Mutiny on the Bounty and Oliver. Kenneth Griffith, born at Tenby, was an enthusiastic controversialist as well as a compelling actor. He was in Only Two Can Play, Wild Geese, A Night to Remember and The Prisoner. Several films he directed were shelved as too provocative. Siân Phillips has played many stage leads and her films include Goodbye Mr Chips and Under Milk Wood. Meredith Edwards was in The Blue Lamp, The Cruel Sea, Dunkirk, The Trials of Oscar Wilde

and Only Two Can Play. Rhondda-born Donald Houston had strong roles in The Blue Lagoon, A Run for Your Money and Room at the Top. Rachel Roberts, from Llanelli, had great impact in Saturday Night and Sunday Morning, and This Sporting Life.

Of a later generation, Margam-born Anthony Hopkins was inspired by Richard Burton and has starred in Young Winston, The Bounty, The Bunker, The Silence of the Lambs, A Bridge Too Far, and The Remains of the Day.

292. Emlyn Williams, c.1975

293. Siân Phillips, c.2001

294. Shirley Bassey, c.1957

295. Anthony Hopkins, c.1993

A VOICE IN THE WORLD

The classic Welsh sound that emerged during the Victorian reinvention of Wales sprang from the amateur choirs of chapels and collieries whose voices were annealed in the unique competitive fire of eisteddfodau. This shared tradition of music and comradeship was a salient feature of life and community in Wales, even if it became stereotypical. It formed the sturdy root of the Welsh National Opera. Indeed, the company had an amateur chorus for the first 22 years of its existence. It was founded by Idloes Owen in 1946, and the pioneering aspect was exemplified in the early years by the spectacle of opera fans with tickets for a WNO performance making their way on horseback to a tent in west Wales.

In its progress from humble birth to international reputation, through many years of penury, it owed much to the enthusiasm of knowledgeable ordinary people who loved their music and musical heroes. The names of some of the stars, Geraint Evans, Stuart Burrows, Gwyneth Jones, Margaret Price, Kenneth Bowen, Della Jones, Gwynne Howell, Robert Tear, Catrin Wyn Davies, Dennis O'Neill, Rebecca Evans and Bryn Terfel, attest the remarkable vigour of the musical tradition in a small country; and the significance of the eisteddfod in developing performers. Emphatically Welsh, a platform for great singers, it tours widely in England with its orchestra and chorus. Its new home in Cardiff's Millennium Centre fulfils a dream. The National Library houses an immense WNO archive of struggle and achievement.

In keeping with the flourishing of music in Wales the Cardiff Singer of the World competition began in 1983 and grew into a fixture in the world music calendar. The BBC Welsh Symphony Orchestra, which became the BBC National Orchestra of Wales, spreads its fame in tours abroad, a cultural force in Wales and a player in the world.

Opera giants:
Sir Geraint Evans,
c.1982, and Bryn Terfel,
c.1997, both portraits
by David Griffiths

296.

297.

AN EASEL IN THE MOUNTAINS

298. *Lle Cul, Patagonia*

Through his dramatic observations of north Wales, depictions of rural characters and penetrating portraits Kyffin Williams made himself a national treasure, his work iconic and much collected. He recalled that when he was disqualified from army service in 1941 the doctors said: 'You are abnormal, we suggest you take up art.' He was art master at Highgate school in London and meanwhile drew on his memories of Anglesey and Snowdonia to create his distinctive and often monumental landscapes of crags, cliffs and stone walls, populated by wind-whipped shepherds, ponies, black and white Border collies and farmers leaning on hazel sticks.

He was criticized for persisting in his Romantic painting of the Welsh landscape but explained that he felt fortunate to paint a world and its people with whom he felt close affinity. 'I can really see no point in doing anything else.' In no other country, he said, had he found the mood that touches a seam within most Welshmen, 'a melancholy deriving from the dark hills, heavy clouds and sea mists.'

In 1968-9, however, he made a notable journey to Patagonia to paint the descendants of the Welsh settlers and their strangely beautiful land. It was pivotal in his career, an exploration of colour and new techniques. 'Images appeared on my canvases different from any I had previously painted.' He produced forty-four remarkable pictures.

299. *The Reynolds family at Lle Cul*

Many of these, with sketches and watercolours, form part of the large collection the artist gave to the National Library over the years. It includes a number of his honest and incisive portraits; he was a shrewd analyst of character. Sir Kyffin returned to his native Anglesey in 1973. He died in 2006, aged eighty-eight.

300.
Kyffin in impish mood: after staying with a friend at Tremadog Kyffin used to draw thank-you cartoons, variations of the comic Crawshay Bailey verses, sung with gusto down the years

Crawshay Bailey's sister Alice Was the cook at Lambeth Palace But she burnt the Bishop's haddock So was sent home to Llangadog.

GALLERY

The sheer breadth of the National Library's reflection of the history and life of Wales is also demonstrated in its enthusiastic commitment to art. The founding charter encouraged the collecting of paintings of people, landscape, villages, churches, chapels and bridges. Today the picture collection comprises more than 5,000 paintings, drawings and topographical prints. It includes work by Augustus John, Gwen John, Kyffin Williams, David Jones, Will Roberts, Josef Herman, John Elwyn, Evan Walters, John Piper, Charles Tunnicliffe, Gwilym Prichard, Peter Prendergast, Claudia Williams, Ivor Davies, Arthur Giardelli, John

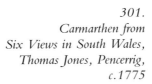

Petts, Vincent Evans, Hywel Harries, Ceri Richards, Donald McIntyre and Aneurin Jones. Earlier works are by Paul Sandby, Penry Williams, Thomas Jones, Pencerrig, Thomas Rowlandson, John Ingleby, John Parker, Peter de Wint and Richard Wilson. Born in 1713, Wilson was the father of Welsh landscape painting. He returned from a spell in Italy in 1756 to cast his native Wales in an Italian glow and his work had a significant influence on later generations. J.M.W. Turner visited Wales often and the collection includes his paintings of Dolbadarn Castle and Aberdulais Mill.

Sandby's aquatints of the mid-eighteenth century were the first published in Britain and the first to show views of Wales to a wide audience. William Daniell, who had made his reputation with his uncle Thomas in India, produced outstanding aquatints of the Welsh coast in 1813. The collection has fine engravings of castles and abbeys made in the 1740s by the brothers Samuel and Nathaniel Buck. There are sixty-three Welsh views painted by the Swiss romantic watercolourist Samuel Hieronymus Grimm during his tour of 1777. Special editions of Thomas Pennant's tours are lavishly illustrated by Moses Griffith and John Ingleby. The collection's portrait archive of political, literary and public figures includes Augustus John's study of Lloyd George.

302.
The Reading Room,
Will Roberts

303. In the Isle of Capri,
near Naples, Thomas Jones,
Pencerrig, 1782

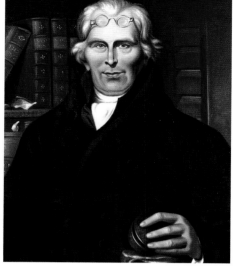

304.
John Williams,
Yr Hen Syr,
William Roos,
1827

305.
Aberdulais Mill,
J.M.W. Turner, c.1796–7

306.
Cofeb
Tryweryn,
John Meirion
Morris, 1998

308.
Propping after
the blast,
Vincent Evans,
1935

307.
Tre'r Ddôl,
John Piper, 1954

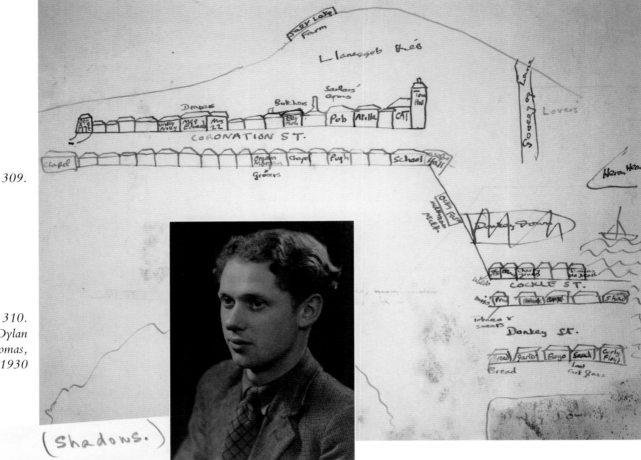

309.

310.
Dylan
Thomas,
c.1930

(Shadows.)

There are shadows in bright sunlight.
Shadows of tall trees on dusty roads
Of village bright church towers, the bells ringing.
Of cattle drinking, their shadows on the midged and
hazy, lazy summer water,
Of sheep angled on white cliffs
Of lambs about their mothers
Of cows in shallow streams, drinking
Of peasant lovers in deep and idle early evening lanes,
Of the jutting and hanging roofs of old houses in a
narrow sunbaked streets,
Of childrens hoops bowling along the cobbles of sunny squares,
Of the piled fruit and striped canvas of open-air
markets, the balloons of street vendors, the awnings
over little shops.
Of large cottage loaves, and large tea pots on white
tea cloths spread on tressel tables under garden trees,
Of the wheels of carriages rolling along a sunlit quay.
Of fishermen making sails on the strand.
Of the sails of boats and ships on sparkling water.
Of the sails and masts and masts of one slowly moving
three masted ship.
And now that ship with its great white sails is rounding
a cliff point towards us.   The high cliffs stand white
against a cloudless sky.   There are long white beeches.

311.

WORKS IN PROGRESS

The National Library's literary archive stores
the work of most of the important Welsh
writers. Letters, handwritten manuscripts
and typescripts give a fascinating insight
into the way in which prose and poetry
take shape. Scribbled afterthoughts,
amendments and crossings-out show
craftsmanship and struggle, the writing
emerging like a figure from a stone under
the sculptor's chisel.

As he composed Under Milk Wood
Dylan Thomas doodled a map to help
him get his bearings in his imagined village
of Llareggub. The large collection of radio
writing in the BBC archive held in the
library has some of Thomas's typed scripts.

312.
Bust of Gwyn Thomas,
Bangor, 2005

313. Mind the bombs:
T.S.Eliot wrote to Idris
Davies, pictured above

314. An intensely private man:
R.S.Thomas,
Kyffin Williams

315. Gwyn Thomas,
1913–1981.
c.1975

316. Alun Lewis,
John Petts

The large and flowing handwriting of
the artist and poet David Jones shows him
working towards completion of his epic
poem In Parenthesis, published in 1937
after years of work punctuated by sickness.
His substantial archive also contains charming
Christmas cards he painted as a child and
many of his sketches and preparatory
drawings. He often agonized over letters
and sometimes wrote half a dozen drafts.

Islwyn Ffowc Elis's exercise books are
filled with the first and only draft of his
stories, all written in a neat hand. The
archive of the Rhymney poet Idris Davies
has a wartime letter from T.S. Eliot, who
worked for Faber, the publisher, advising
Davies to 'copy your poems in case of
bombing.' In Eliot's view Idris Davies wrote
'the best poetic document I know about a
particular epoch in a particular place.' Among
other literary papers acquired by the library
are those of the Welsh-language writers
Saunders Lewis, W.J. Gruffydd, T.H. Parry-
Williams, R.Williams Parry, T. Gwynn Jones,
Marion Eames and Angharad Tomos; and
the Anglo-Welsh authors Vernon Watkins,
Brenda Chamberlain, Jan Morris, Edward
Thomas, Gwyn Thomas, Glyn Jones, Roland
Mathias, Alun Lewis, John Cowper Powys,
Harri Webb and Gillian Clarke. There is
a large archive of the manuscripts of the
prolific Emyr Humphreys, who writes
in both languages.

IN THIS PLACE

No National Library existed in Wales in Iolo Morganwg's lifetime. He nevertheless scribbled a hopeful note to the future, bequeathing his manuscripts to the library 'when founded.' In 1873, forty-seven years after his death, a library campaign started at the National Eisteddfod in Mold, the first determined step towards realizing the dream. King Edward VII granted the charter on 19 March 1907. George V and Queen Mary laid the foundation stone on

the twenty-acre hilltop site in 1911. The architect was Sidney Greenslade. Entitled under the Copyright Act to claim every British book, newspaper and periodical published, the library received its first copies in 1912. Staff and readers occupied the first blocks of the structure in 1916. Queen Elizabeth II opened the main building in 1955.

From the beginning the library has been in a state of expansion and is today

317. Foundation day: King George V and Queen Mary, Princess Mary and the newly-invested Prince of Wales, at the foundation stone ceremony of The National Library of Wales, 15 July 1911. The king laid the first stone and the queen the second

Left: The king lays the founding granite stone; and right: John Ballinger, the Librarian, Sidney Greenslade, the architect, Evan Davies Jones, chairman of the building

committee and Sir John Williams, the Library President, with the American ambassador, Whitelaw Reid, inspect progress on the building in November 1912

318.

319.

in the throes of the accelerating digital revolution, an advance in communications as profound as Gutenberg's press five centuries ago. The gateway function of traditional publishers is changing rapidly in a liberated on-line world where anyone can publish anything. All libraries have to confront the problems of what to select from the vast array of digital information and how to store it.

The National Library of Wales also has to meet its unusual and wider obligations as a totally bilingual knowledge service; as a national gallery with a broad collection of portraits and topographical pictures and a need to exhibit them effectively; and as a sound and vision collector. A century after its founding the task is infinitely more varied, complex and exciting, but remains the same: telling the story of Wales.

Out of the World.

MISS ABERYSTWYTH: Boo-oo-oo; I want the National Library!

DAME CARDIFF: Hadn't you better wait, dear, until flying machines are a practicability?

320. The rivals: Joseph Staniforth's Western Mail cartoon shows Cardiff and Aberystwyth competing for The National Library of Wales

Chronology

c.589   Death of Saint David.
  878   Death of Rhodri Mawr.
  950   Death of Hywel Dda.
 1176   Eisteddfod at Cardigan.
 1188   Giraldus Cambrensis journeys
        through Wales.
 1282   Death of Llywelyn II.
 1283   Edward I begins building major castles.
 1284   Statute of Rhuddlan.
c.1320 Dafydd ap Gwilym born.
 1400   Revolt of Owain Glyn Dŵr.
 1485   Henry Tudor lands in Wales, takes
        the crown at Bosworth.
 1530   Population of Wales c.230,000.
 1536   Acts of Union, assimilation of Wales
        into England.
 1536   Dissolution of religious houses begins.
 1546   First printed book in Welsh.
 1567   New Testament and Prayer Book
        published in Welsh.
 1573   Humphrey Llwyd's map of Wales.
 1588   Bishop Morgan's Welsh Bible.
 1682   Welsh Quakers flee to Pennsylvania.
 1695   Printing press restrictions lifted.
 1731   Griffith Jones begins literacy campaign.
 1735   Conversion of Howel Harris.
 1744   William Williams Pantycelyn
        publishes first hymns.
 1751   Honourable Society of Cymmrodorion
        founded in London.
 1751   Population of Wales c. 490,000.
 1782   Lord Penrhyn begins slate industry in
        north Wales.
 1792   Iolo Morganwg's first Gorsedd,
        London.
 1797   French landing at Fishguard.
 1801   First census: population of Wales
        587,000.
 1804   Richard Trevithick runs steam
        locomotive at Merthyr.
 1805   Ann Griffiths hymns published.

 1811   Welsh Methodists
        secede from Church of England.
 1819   Eisteddfod at Ivy Bush, Carmarthen.
 1826   Telford completes Menai
        suspension bridge.
 1831   Merthyr workers' uprising.
 1839   Chartists march on Newport.
 1839   Rebecca riots.
 1839   Marquis of Bute's dock opens
        at Cardiff.
 1841   Taff Vale railway opens.
 1847   Blue Books education report.
 1851   Population of Wales 1.16 million.
 1855   First steam coal taken from Rhondda
        to Cardiff.
 1856   Evan and James James compose
        Hen Wlad Fy Nhadau.
 1865   Welsh colony founded in Patagonia.
 1868   Liberal victory in 'great election.'
 1869   Western Mail founded.
 1872   University of Wales opens
        at Aberystwyth.
 1881   Welsh Rugby Union founded.
 1883   Opening of University College Cardiff.
 1886   Tithe riots.
 1889   David Davies opens Barry Docks.
 1890   David Lloyd George elected MP
        for Caernarfon Boroughs.
 1893   Welsh Labour Party founded.
 1896   Collapse of Cymru Fydd.
 1898   South Wales Miners' Federation
        founded.
 1900   Great strike begins at Penrhyn quarry.
 1900   Keir Hardie elected at Merthyr as first
        Independent Labour MP.

Acknowledgements

The writing of this centenary volume for The National Library of Wales gave me a unique opportunity to explore the nation's story. I am grateful for all the help I received. I should like to express my thanks to Andrew Green, the Librarian, and to his staff, past and present, who assisted, advised and educated me and patiently sought out documents, books and illustrations. Geraint Talfan Davies and Dr Brinley Jones commented most helpfully on the narrative. It was also my good fortune to work with Olwen Fowler, designer of distinction.

References for images in this volume

The National Library of Wales gratefully acknowledges the copyright permission granted by copyright holders. Every effort has been made to contact copyright holders for each item listed. If any image has been reproduced without the permission of the copyright holder we apologise and will rectify the omission in any future edition. Except where otherwise indicated, copyright of the images used rests with The National Library of Wales.

JT = John Thomas Collection
GC= Geoff Charles Collection
NSSAW= The National Screen and Sound Archive of Wales

Opposite title page: 'Tir y Blaenau' David Jones c.1924-5, PB8681 ©Anthony Hyne
Title Page: Photo anon, John Ballinger (right), Sir John Williams (seated) and two unidentified individuals in North Reading Room. NLW Acc. No. 4800/26, NLW Photo Album 835/26
Contents page: Tabernacl Chapel, Porthmadog, tea party, NLW Photo Album 2107, PG5966/90; Image from the 'Jerry the Troublesome Tyke' series (Pathe, 1925-1927), courtesy of British Pathe plc. NSSAW
Opposite Foreword: T H Parry-Williams, PE 832; Rev. Francis Kilvert, PG1074/76; R. Williams Parry, PB8855(2); Waldo Williams, PB7904; 'Aberglaslyn Pass' Thomas Prydderch, 1920, 199600048
Opposite Preface: Front elevation of The National Library of Wales; Royal Charter granted 19 March 1907

1. NLW Acc. No. PG3749; © Estate of Sir Kyffin Williams/ Licensed by DACS 2007; **2.** NLW Acc. No. PE3093; © Estate of Sir Kyffin Williams/ Licensed by DACS 2007; **3.** NLW Acc. No. PE3733; **4.** NLW Photo Album 858; **5.** NLW Drawing volume 56, no.11; **6.** NLW Acc. No. PB 3066a; **7.** NLW Drawing volume 300, no. 85 i; **8.** NLW Acc. No. CE590/49; **9.** NLW Paper Money Collection; **10.** NLW Acc. No. PA3416; **11.** Illustrated London News, 20 Feb 1875; **12.** Photo by Stephen Timothy NLW Photo Album 1826; **13.** A Duncan, L Godfrey, NLW Acc. No. PB7527; **14.** NLW Acc. No. PB2533; **15.** NLW Acc. No. PA9325; **16.** Peniarth MS 28, f. 15v; **17.** Peniarth MS 28, f. 21v; **18.** NLW BV 407, p. 50; **19.** NLW Acc. No.199804702; **20.** Peniarth MS 481, f. 51v; **21.** Peniarth MS 20, p. 292; **22.** NLW Acc. No. PB 9246; **23.** NLW Photo Album 2002; **24.** Picture from Owain Glyndŵr, 2000 © published by Y Lolfa; **25.** Picture from Land of My Fathers, Hodder & Stoughton, 1915; **26.** NLW Acc. No. PB8119; **27.** NLW Map 1003; **28.** Great Sessions 94/17/15; **29.** NLW Acc. No. P783; **30.** NLW Acc. No. P506; **31.** NLW Acc. No. PG399 © Keith Bowen; **33.** NLW Drawing volume 56, no.1; **34.** JT/J18; **35.** NLW Acc. No. 200306685; **36.** JT/BB52; **39.** NLW Acc. No. PG 471; **40.** NLW Acc. No.199700099; **41.** NLW Acc. No. PD6886; **42.** NLW Acc. No. CB6254; **43.** NLW Acc. No. PE288 © Estate of John Petts; **44.** JT/H70; **45.** NLW Acc. No. PB3508; **46.** Published by W. Owen, 1849, NLW Acc. No. PB2528; **47.** NLW Photo Album 1862; **48.** NLW Photo Album 1861; **49.** NLW Photo Album 1862; **50.** NLW Photo Album 3003; **51.** Photo by Francis Frith, NLW Acc. No. PG5125/642, NLW Photo Album 2009;

52. NLW Photo Album 936; **53.** NLW Acc. No. PE4434 © Ronald H.J Lawrence; **54.** NLW Photo Album 990; **55.** NLW Photo Album 1863; **56.** NLW Photo Album 1863; **57.** Photo anon, NLW Photo Album 1323; **58.** NLW Acc. No. PZ617/12; **59.** NLW Photo Album 2101; **60.** Published R E Jones & Bros, Conway, NLW Photo Album 2306; **61.** NLW Photo Album 102; **62.** JT/E84; **63.** NLW Photo Album 2435 © Paul White; **64.** NLW Photo Album 2433 © Paul White; **65.** Photo anon, NLW Photo Album 2100; **66.** Photo by Weekly Illustrated cameraman, 11 January 1936, p.13; **67.** NLW Photo Album 3684; **68.** NLW Acc. No. PG5920/107, NLW Photo Album 2100; **69.** GC/C1507; **70.** GC/A39/47/E28; **71.** GC/A39/45/B31; **72.** NLW Acc. No. PA8087, NLW Photo Album 875 © South Wales Evening Post; **73.** GC/T22; **74.** GC/T63; **75.** Photo by Raymond Daniel, NLW Photo Album 3898; **76.** Photo by Julian Sheppard, NLW Photo Album 4151; **77.** Photo by Raymond Daniel, NLW Photo Album 3898; **78.** Photo by Raymond Daniel, NLW Acc. No. 200310480/47/28; **79.** NLW Acc. No. 13599069/9 © Ron Davies; **80.** NLW Photo Album 1065 © Ken Davies, Carmarthen; **81.** NLW Photo Album 588 © Martin Shakeshaft; **82.** GC/A/49/17/F35; **83.** NLW Acc. No. PE 3584 ©Valerie Ganz; **84.** NLW Photo Album 4529 © David Williams/ Photolibrary Wales; **85.** NLW Acc. No. 020001827/29, NLW Photo Album 3139, © Jeremy Moore; **86.** NLW Map 1002, NLW Acc. No. PB1129; **87.** Peniarth MS 1, f. 4r; **88.** Peniarth MS 1, ff. 1r, 9r, 24r, 53r; **89.** Peniarth MS 1, f. 29v; **90.** Peniarth MS 23, f. 75v; **91.** NLW Acc. No. PB8678 © Anthony Hyne; **92.** NLW Acc. No. PG2488; **93.** Peniarth MS 4, f. 1r; **94.** Peniarth MS 28, f. 6v; **95.** Peniarth MS 28, f. 20v; **96.** Peniarth MS 28, f. 1v; **97.** Peniarth MS 28, f. 6r; **98.** Peniarth MS 28, f. 5r; **99.** Peniarth MS 2, f. 3v; **100.** NLW MS 6680B, f. 121r; **101.** NLW MS 7006D, p. 198; **102.** NLW MS 7006D; **103.** NLW MS 3024C, ff. 3v-4r; **104.** NLW Acc. No. PG79; **105.** Photo anon, NLW Photo Album 863; **106.** Peniarth MS 392, f. 2; **107.** NLW MS 17520A, ff. 4v, 3r, 2r; **108.** NLW Acc. No. 1855, P5712; **109.** NLW MS 22631C, f. 96; **110.** NLW MS 735C, ff. 21r, 19v, 10v, 14v; **111.** Peniarth MS 1, f. 36r; **112.** NLW MS 20541E, f. 204; **113.** Peniarth MS 135, p. 60; **114.** NLW MS 3026C, p. 26; **115.** NLW MS 3026C, pp. 28, 11, 16; **116.** Peniarth MS 194; **117.** Bettisfield 202; **121.** Peniarth MS 267, f. 11; **122.** NLW MS 9095B, p. 29; **124.** NLW Map Ab1043, engraved title-page; **125.** NLW Map Ab1043 no.18; **126.** NLW Map 1003; **127.** Great Sessions 14/14, f. 161; **128.** Great Sessions 4/617/2/23; **130.** NLW MS 21834B, f.i; **132.** NLW Acc. No. PA10022; **133.** Photo by Elwyn Jenkins, Llandovery, NLW Photo Album 1496; **134.** Portrait Acc. No. PZ6210; chair CMA exhibition item 3; **136.** NLW Acc. No. PB8962; **137.** NLW MS 694D; **138.** NLW Acc. No. PA6243; **139.** CMA 16234, ff. 57-8; **140.** NLW Acc. No. PG 881; **141.** NLW BV 407, p.12; **142.** NLW Acc No. CR 4672ii; **143.** NLW Acc No. CR4672ii; **144.** NLW Acc No. PD9867; **145.** NLW MS 12706E; **146.** NLW Acc No. CR 4672ii; **147.** NLW Posters Collection; **148.** NLW Acc No. P1142; **149.** NLW Acc No. P5283; **150.** NLW Acc. No. P8839; **151.** NLW Acc. No. PA5328; **152.** NLW MS 21420E; **154.** NLW Box 28 (Port.A); **155.** NLW Rolls 108; **157.** NLW Acc. No. PB2471; **158.** NLW Posters Collection; **159.** JT/KK56; **160.** JT/B064; **161.** NLW Paper Money collection;

162. Glansevern 14059; **163.** GC/T76; **164.** NLW Coll. XSF; **165.** JT/J60; **166.** JT/K21; **167.** Photo by P.B. Abery, NLW Robert Owen Coll. R003; **168.** NLW Acc. No. Pos 22/39 PY518; **169.** NLW Acc. No. Pos 23/15, PY532; inset NLW Acc. No. P5262; **170.** Cambrian Newspaper report trial of Dic Penderyn, August 1831; **171.** NLW Acc. No. PZ3211; **172.** Francis Frith, NLW Photo Album 2036; **173.** JT/G93; **174.** GC/R267; **175.** Llandinam Collection 87/88; **176.** Ladd and Co., NLW Photo Album 1861; **177.** NLW Acc. No. PG 8532; **178.** JT/K29; **179.** JT/M40; **180.** NLW BV 407, p.202; **181.** NLW BV 407, p.154; **182.** Photo anon, NLW Photo Album 858; **183.** JT/H71; **184.** NLW Acc. No. PE3408; **185.** Rev. Calvert Richard Jones. PG726, NLW Photo Album 1074; **186.** JT/JJ71; **187.** JT/KK57; **188.** JT/KK15; **189.** JT/KK20; **190.** JT/KK84; **191.** JT/CC27; **192.** JT/BB031; **193.** JT/KK41; **194.** JT/KK72; **195.** JT/KK19; **196.** NLW Photo Album 3900, no.37; **197.** H.M. Allen, NLW Photo Album 243; **198.** GC/C8588/1; **199.** NLW Photo Album 4201; **200.** Evan James 1, f. 41v; **201.** NLW Acc. No. PE3776; **202.** NLW Acc. No. PE3777; **203.** NLW Acc. No. 200410970, NLW Photo Album 4123; **204.** NLW Acc. No. PB7649, NLW Photo Album 2416; **205.** NLW Facs 856; **206.** NLW Photo Album 2146; **208.** NLW Drawing volume 299; **209.** JT/V56A; **210.** NLW Folder 184; **213.** NLW Acc. No. PE385/4; **215.** NLW Drawing volume 275a, p.152; **216.** NLW Drawing volume 275a, p.206; **217.** NLW Drawing volume 275a, p.104; **218.** NLW MS 22090A, f. 76 © Sheila Hooper; **219.** NLW Acc. No. 3289; **220.** NLW Acc. No. PB3802; **221.** NLW Acc. No. PB6593; **222.** NLW Acc. No. 200312819/12, NLW Photo Album 3904; **223.** NLW Acc. No. PZ3697; **226.** NLW Acc. No. CR4672ii; **227.** NLW Acc. No. PZ3606; **228.** NLW Acc. No. PZ5092; **229.** NLW Photo Album 4287 © Western Mail & Echo; **230.** NLW Photo Album 4287 © Sports & General Press Agency/ EMPICS; **231.** NLW John Charles Collection © The Press Association / EMPICS; **232.** NLW Acc. No. PB9133/44, NLW Drawing volume 275; **233.** NLW Acc. No. PZ6754/13; **235.** NLW Photo Album 3140 © Jeremy Moore; **236.** NLW Photo Album 962; **237.** JT/D76; **238.** NLW Acc. No. PZ5677; **239.** Photo by Wickens, Bangor, NLW Photo Album 1323; **240.** NLW Acc. No. PB4671 © Artists Estate/ Bridgeman Art Library; **241.** JT/K45; **243.** NLW Acc. No. PG3089/28, NLW Photo Album 1224; **244.** NLW MS 20429C, (1336iii); **245.** NLW MS 20419C, (823i); **246.** NLW Acc. No. PG5451/11, NLW Photo Album 1923 © Mo Wilson; **247.** Photo by William Benton, NLW Photo Album 1863, no.19; **248.** Photo by William Benton, NLW Photo Album 1863, no.15; **249.** Photo by William Benton, NLW Photo Album 1863, no.6; **250.** Still courtesy of the British Film Institute, copy in the collection of NSSAW; **251.** NLW ex 1806; **252.** NLW ex 1806; **253.** NLW ex 1806; **254.** NLW ex 1806; **255.** GC/C3273; **256.** NLW Acc. No. PB7387 (Port. A); **257.** GC/C3275; **258.** Photo by Wickens, Bangor, NLW Acc. No. PA2466 (Port. A); **259.** Photo by Julian Shepherd, NLW Photo Album 4152; **260.** NLW MS 22723D, p. 5 © Plaid Cymru; **261.** Kate Roberts Collection 2136 © Plaid Cymru; **262.** NSSAW collection; **263.** NLW Object Collection; **265.** Photograph by Anthony Buckley, NLW Acc. No. PB6734, © Kenneth Hughes; **266.** Gardner & Co., NLW Acc. No. SD593; **267.** Andre & Sleigh, NLW Acc. No. 199905542, NLW Photo Album 1036; **268.** Photo anon, NLW Acc.

No. PB8962; **269.** Photo anon, NLW Acc. No. PG986; **270.** © Hughes a'i Fab, by permission of S4C; **271.** GC/M/1086/C22; **272.** GC/M/725/C23; **273.** GC/C2279; **274.** NLW MS 22424F; **275.** NLW MS 22424F; **276.** PG3807/1-5, NLW Photo Album 1054 © National Museum Wales; **277.** NLW Archive Coll. Negs 2067 o,p; 2072 c-gg; **278.** GC/M72/C10; **279.** Photo by Raymond Daniel, NLW Acc. No. 200310480/48/3A; **280.** © S4C; **281.** © S4C; **282.** NLW ILW 3245 © Solo Syndication/ Associated Newspapers; **283.** NLW ILW 4369 © Solo Syndication/ Associated Newspapers **284.** NLW Acc. No. 200300351, NLW Photo Album 3850 © Bryn Campbell; **285.** © Western Mail & Echo Ltd.; **286.** GC/E65/238; **287.** GC/C1874; **288.** GC/E65C/34; **289.** Photo by Norman Greyspeerdt, NLW Acc. No. 00304158/1, NLW Photo Album 1807 © Rank Organisation; **290.** NLW Acc. No. 199700082, NLW Photo Album 1807; **291.** Still from 'Dylan Thomas' (1962) a Jack Howells film in the collection of NSSAW; **292.** Photo anon, NLW Acc. No. PG5409/242, NLW Photo Album 1904; **293.** NLW Acc. No. 200112675, NLW Photo Album 1807 © Mike Martin; **294.** Photo anon, NLW Acc. No. 199902158. NLW Photo Album 3087; **295.** NLW Acc. No. PG4376, NLW Photo Album 1783 © Siân Trenberth; **296.** NLW Acc. No. PE2837 © David Griffiths; **297.** NLW Acc. No.199800295 © David Griffiths; **298.** NLW Acc. No. PG4824 © Estate of Kyffin Williams / Licensed by DACS 2007; **299.** NLW Acc. No. PB7122 © Estate of Kyffin Williams / Licensed by DACS 2007; **300.** NLW Acc. No. PZ3146 © Estate of Kyffin Williams / Licensed by DACS 2007; **301.** NLW Acc. No. PD00308, NLW BV 202; **302.** NLW Acc. No. 200202336 © Sian Roberts; **303.** NLW Acc. No. PG00447; **304.** NLW Acc. No. PA8159; **305.** NLW Acc. No.199700329; **306.** NLW Acc. No. 200404144 © John Meirion Morris; **307.** NLW Acc. No. 200208586 © Estate of John Piper; **308.** NLW Acc. No. 200004331 © Audrey Lane; **309.** NLW MS 23949D © David Higham Associates; **310.** NLW Photo Album 1925; **311.** NLW MS 20666C; **312.** NLW 2006 accession © John Meirion Morris; **313.** NLW MS 22415C © Faber & Faber Ltd.; **314.** NLW Acc. No. 199900979 © Estate of Sir Kyffin Williams / Licensed by DACS 2007; **315.** Photo Julian Shepherd, NLW Acc. No,2005000235/297, NLW Photo Album 4153; **316.** NLW Acc. No. PG492 © Estate of John Petts; **317.** NLW Archive 57; **318.** NLW Archive 57; **319.** NLW Acc. No. PE132, NLW Photo Album 1054; **320.** NLW Drawing volume 275a, p.127.

Chronology: Siân Phillip y Mynydd, JT/KK84; Catherine Zeta-Jones in 'Chicago' © BMG Music Entertainment (US) Ltd.

Acknowledgements: Urdd Gobaith Cymru Coll. 311; Urdd Gobaith Cymru Coll. 323; Newspaper cuttings, NLW ex 1806

Index: 'King and Eddie Scribbins,' 1986, NLW Acc. No. PE5538 © Valerie Ganz; 'The Volunteer at Aberdovey Regatta', c. 1885, photo by John Thomas, JTB018

Front door of The National Library of Wales, detail.

For further information regarding our collections
please visit our website
www.llgc.org.uk

Index

Index compiled by Penny Symon

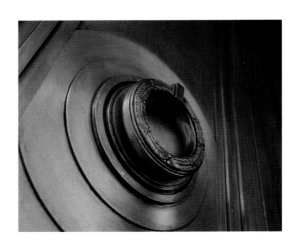